T0365634

A Guide to 3rd Reich Cutlery, its Monograms, Logos and Maker Marks

with
Extensive Historical Exposition

by

James A. Yannes

Order this book online at www.trafford.com
or email orders@trafford.com

Most Trafford titles are also available at major online book retailers.

Note for Librarians: A cataloguing record for this book is available from Library
and Archives Canada at www.collectionscanada.ca/amicus/index-e.html

Printed in Victoria, BC, Canada.

ISBN: 978-1-4269-2678-5 (sc)
ISBN: 978-1-4269-2679-2 (hc)

Library of Congress Control Number: 2010901385

*Our mission is to efficiently provide the world's finest, most comprehensive
book publishing service, enabling every author to experience success.
To find out how to publish your book, your way, and have it available
worldwide, visit us online at www.trafford.com*

Trafford rev. 07/13/2010

www.trafford.com

North America & international
toll-free: 1 888 232 4444 (USA & Canada)
phone: 250 383 6864 ♦ fax: 812 355 4082

3

Table of Contents

Preface

The focus of this book is to expose the reader to the broadest view of the unique markings found on 3rd Reich cutlery and to explore their significance and the historical period in which they were created. The markings we are addressing are the multitude of individual monograms, logos, shields etc. that identify the actual users. The obvious question from an American is why were there so many distinct types? One answer is that the German's felt that small unit cohesion was very desirable and therefore tried to emphasize the individuality of groups to create such a feeling of importance. My first book on the subject entitled *"Collectible Spoons of the 3rd Reich"* was narrowly focused on spoon markings. As my collecting continued, it became obvious that there was more to life than just spoons. As it turns out, spoons are the largest community of cutlery and therefore the easiest to acquire. Spoons, of course, are in every table setting and gift sets of spoons were very popular. Typically, spoons tend to be an item to accumulate attested to by the existence of commemorative spoons. Forks on the other hand are in relatively short supply, in my experience probably one fork for every 5 spoons available but typically at a lower price than a companion spoon. The knife is the orphan of the table. A knife collection would be virtually impossible to put together as they are normally available only in place settings which are few and proportionately expensive plus I have never seen a knife display rack whereas spoon / fork racks are in abundance.

The German word BESTECK is defined as including Knives, Spoons and Forks and its English translation is CUTLERY. English has a number of descriptors for Besteck including cutlery, silverware, tableware and flatware. I will stick with cutlery.

Devices found on 3rd Reich Cutlery

There are 3 major cutlery types defined by their basic material for which devices are required and which appear on the cutlery's reverse.

First are the 'silver' cutlery'. Here the cutlery is composed of a mixture of silver and copper. The most common German decimal silver standard marks are 800 and 925 and attest to the proportion of the silver as 80% and 92.5% (sterling) with the remainder copper. German laws required the stamp of either 800 or 925 on the reverse of the spoon. There are also 830, 835, 900, and 935 to be found.

Second are silver plated cutlery. Here the basic cutlery is typically made of 'German Silver" with a plating of pure silver. Per contemporary Wellner & WMF inputs, silver plating is only done using pure silver. The most popular plating indicator is the number 90. If, as an example, a '90' appears, it indicates, per Wellner, that 90 grams (3.2 oz) of silver is applied per a surface area of 24 quadradezimeters, equivalent to 24 cutlery pieces (6 each: teaspoons, tablespoons, knives and forks). WMF states the '90' is 90 grams of silver plate on 24 square decimeters = 372 square inches which corresponds to the surface of 24 menu spoons. Plating numbers can go as low as 30 for hotel ware and up. And when alone, can be in either a circle, a square or a stand alone. Currently, WMF offers up to 150!

There are plated cutlery with not only silver plating signs but also style signs. In this case, the silver plate is typically listed inside a circle. The style number follows and is inside a square. Both Wellner and WMF attested to this marking scheme.

Third is cutlery which is neither 'silver' nor silver plated. their base material is typically aluminum, stainless steel or alpacca (German silver).

Typical markings / materials include:
Alpacca - see pages 33 & 221
Aluminium = aluminum
Rustfrei = Rust Free (Stainless Steel)
Nicht Rostend = None Rusting
Gusstahl Solingen = Cast Steel
Tomback = an alloy of copper and zinc. Replaced during the late war with pure zinc
Cupal: Aluminum between two thin sheets of copper. Usually surface plated with silver or gilt.
Leichtmetall or Lightweight alloy
Kriegsmetall or War Metal, a poor quality alloy of zinc, copper and lead. Commonly called Pot Metal by collectors.

It was not uncommon when applying personal monograms to cutlery, to only apply it to the major pieces such as the spoons, forks and knives and to leave the minor pieces clear of the monogram. (saving money??)

Almost all cutlery will carry a Herstellerkennzeichen or Makers Mark or Manufacturers ID on the reverse. This can be the name of the manufacturer: "Bruckmann" or the manufacturers initials or a mark such as Wellner's die in a circle. Unfortunately, many makers marks remain a mystery as the original registries have been lost or destroyed. Surprisingly, for a nation famous for its organization, there does not appear to be a directory of 3rd Reich era makers marks!

German Law regarding Maker's Marks

In 1884 a law was enacted making .800 the minimum national standard in Germany for silver. In 1886 the use of individual city marks was abolished and replaced by the national mark (Reichsmark or RM) of a crescent moon & crown (Halbmond und Krone) representing the entire German state. These marks became compulsory by 1888. The Crescent Moon & Crown are used in conjunction with a decimal silver standard mark, usually .800 or .925 and a maker's mark. Due to the large number of manufacturers and an apparent lack of centralized records, many maker's marks can no longer be identified.

This eagle is a Bruckmann & Sohne maker's mark, manufacturers ID, hallmark, herstellerkennzeichen or herstellerpunzierungen

The Cutlery is organized into sections.

Section I - Personalities

Cutlery associated with specific personalities. In some cases the flatware carries the initials of the owner and in others, a pattern strictly associated with a specific person and is typically applied to the obverse.. The easy examples are the Adolf Hitler spoons marked with his personal eagle straddled with his initials "A" and "H". In the absence of initials, at times the Eagle is the key., von Ribbontrop's eagle is very similar to Hitler's but unique as is Bormann's. Another identifier would be a Hans Frank spoon which carries the / his official state pattern of the Governor General of Poland.   These pieces are usually listed by the associated owners name.

Included are representational pieces from:

Adolf Hitler
Eva Braun
Herman Goering
Heinrich Himmler
Albert Speer
Helmut Weidling
Bernard Rust
Dr. Robert Ley
Ernst Kaltenbrunner
Fritz Sauckel
Hans Frank
Bishop Ludwig Mueller
Martin Bormann
Joachim von Ribbentrop
Rudolf Hess
Reinhard Heydrich

Section II - Other Government

Under the 3rd Reich, essentially all organizations were either in the government or were eliminated, the labor unions being a prime example. Organizational cutlery typically carries the Logo of the organization on the obverse. Included are representational pieces from:

N.S.D.A.P. - Nationalsozialistische Deutsche
     Arbeiterpartei, (National Socialist German
     Worker's Party)

SA - Sturmabteilung - Storm troopers

DJV - Deutsche Jungvolk - German Youth

HJ - Hitler Jugend - Hitler Youth

DAF - Deutsche Arbeitfront - German Labor Front

DLV - Deutscher Luftfahrt Verband - German Aviation
     League

DR - Deutsche Reichsbahn - German National
     Railways

DRK - Deutsches Rotes Kreuz - German Red Cross

NSDStB - National Socialistische Studenten Bund -
     National Socialist Student Association

NSKK - NS Kraftfahrkorps - Motor Corps

NSKOV - NS-Kriegsopferversorgung - War Victums
     Welfare Service (WWI)

NSV - NS Volkswohlfahrt - NS People's Welfare

RAD - Reichs Arbeitsdienst - National Labor Service,

RK - (Neu) Reichkanzlei - New National Chancellery,
     Berlin

RKB - Reichskolonialbund - Colonial League

RLB - Reichs Luftschutzbund - National Air Raid
     Protection League

RMJ - Reichministerium der Justiz - Ministry of Justice

RNS - Reichs Nahrstand - Food Estate

Section V - Miscellaneous

Adolf Hitler Napkin Ring
Fuhrerbau's Italian Service
Gastehaus Reichsparteitag
Deutsche Hof Hotel
Bayerischer Hof Hotel
Hotel Post, Berchtesgaden
Dietrich Eckart Krankenhaus
U-47 commemorative
Danziger Werf
Haus der Deutschen Arbeit 1933
House of German Art, 1937
Staatskasino
Kasino Lamsdorf
Rabbit Breeders Association
Danzig Andenken
Nurnberg Andenken
LZ 129 Hindenburg
America's Swastika
Wellner of East Germany
Mystery Fork - GTPp
Mystery Fork - FBCM 41
Mystery - Pre 1886?

INTRODUCTION

In a recent visit to Munich, we came across a "Third Reich Tour". This was a walking tour which "covers all important facts and sites that played a role in the origin of this black chapter, that ended with the beautiful city of Munich in ruins." With a sub title, "Hitler's Munich.". When we asked the tour guide if he was comfortable with the subject matter, he explained that he had been born in the mid 1960's and that for him, the Second World War was history. He said his grand parents and his parents wanted nothing to do with memories of the war. We even have a friend who was born in the late 1930's and baptized 'Adolf' who had his name changed out of revulsion for what had occurred. This encounter brought to mind the changed opinion of Napoleon who had caused the deaths of millions and was condemned by the world in the mid 19th century only to now be a hero of France. This is not to say that Hitler and the 3rd Reich will ever be revered like Napoleon but that as time passes, perceptions dim and places and items take on a historical patina.

There are a number of very interesting Third Reich locations available to anyone with an interest in the historical aspects of what will undoubtedly be the defining military effort in history. My wife and I have visited all the sites to be mentioned but unfortunately when we made our visits, I had no intention of writing about them so the descriptions will be from memory and with little detail.

Munich: This is a good place to start as Hitler called Munich the "Capital of the Movement". There are two walking tours, the two and one half hour "Third Reich Tour" and a 5 hour "Extended Third Reich Tour". I highly recommend a down town hotel so you can walk to the start point in the Marienplatz. Much of the "Nazi" architecture has survived

such as the The Fuhrerbau which is now a music school but
no longer open to the public - the place where Chamberlin
received his 'Peace in our time' paper from Hitler and its
mirror image, the Administration building. Also the
Feldherrnhalle (Field Marshals' Hall) where the 9 Nov 1923
"Beer Hall Putsch" was put down.   A one day side trip to Bad
Wiessee to visit the site of Hitler's arrest of SA leader Ernst
Rohm as depicted in a History Channel episode. The hotel
has been renamed 'Hotel Lederer am See' on Tegernseer
Tal. The staff is not interested in discussing the matter but
there is a very pleasant bar overlooking the lake for cake
and coffee.

Dresden: The Munchner Platz Memorial. This was a central
execution site where some 1,300 were beheaded by
guillotine. A short drive away is Pirna's Sonnenstein
Memorial at Struppener Strasse 22 where some 13,720
mentally ill and retarded patients were gassed - legally -
under "Action T4." T4 is short form for Tiergartenstrasse 4.
the headquarters address,

Wunsdorf: This area south of Berlin has historically been the
headquarters for the Army Command. The idea was to keep
the military out of Berlin proper so as to isolate the political
center from the military center. Here was the Zeppelin
communications bunker, the teletype and telephone
exchange for the army command and Wehrmacht
transportation corps. Also the Maybach Bunker complex for
Army command staff and the "Winkel" air raid shelters.
Tours here are 1.5 hours or special tours of 5 hours. The
tour center is at Gutenbergstrasse 1. Note: As per W.W.II
agreements, the Maybach bunker complex was blown up by
the Russians but they kept the Zeppelin bunker for its
communications as it was felt to be atomic bomb survivable.

Wewelsburg: This triangular castle (one of only 3 in the world) was the ritual headquarters of the SS. It has an extensive museum, well worth the trip.

Quedlinburg: The cathedral was taken over by the SS and in 1937, the bones of King Heinrich I (875-936) were interred. Heinrich Himmler reportedly believed he was the reincarnation of King Heinrich. Himmler visited the tomb periodically and communed with the King who had defeated the Slavs.

So much for travel suggestions.

My first disclaimer: I am not an expert on 3rd Reich cutlery! In fact, I am not really a collector. I am an accumulator. My interests change with time and several years ago I bought a Hitler spoon and used it for several years in my morning coffee. Then I saw an Eva Braun spoon and it seemed appropriate to join them together. This led to picking up various spoons over the years. As it is obvious, my collection is a type collection, with emphasis on breadth rather than depth. As a rank amateur, I have relied on my sources to deliver correct material. So I challenge the reader to point out the inevitable fakes. The intent of the book is to broaden the coverage of this interesting area. Why cutlery? My book entitled, "*Collectible Spoons of the 3rd Reich*" which was published in 2009 was focused on spoons. It recently dawned on me that the book should focus on the variety of markings / monograms on the cutlery and to limit the scope to spoons would leave out many variations that may be only available in forks and knives. For the collector, it is important to be aware of the scope of unique monograms on 3rd Reich cutlery. Being aware of a monogram on cutlery was not the issue, the issue is identifying the monogram. Therefore, forks and knives have been added which have unique monograms. To summarize, spoons and forks are friendly, non threatening utensils and easily displayed. They also entice their collection, both obvious and clandestine. Thomas Breyette, the author of the definitive book on German Tank Destruction Badges told me the story of one of the recipients of the TDB purloining one of Adolf Hitler's spoons as he (the most junior officer in attendance) was the last to retire from his award luncheon hosted by the Fuhrer.

Regarding "Hitler's" personal flatware variations: The only reference books I have are, _Treasure Trove - The Looting of the Third Reich_ by Charles E. Snyder, Jr. Major USAF (Retired) and _"Liberated" Adolf Hitler Memorabilia_ by Mark D. Griffith, M.D. In the Griffith book on page 15 he illustrates and states "close-up of the handles illustrating five of the six different patterns of silverware." where as Snyder illustrates 16 different patterns on pages 37 to 41. As always, these types of inquiries will remain somewhat of a mystery as the records no longer exist. As an example, I purchased a Kriegsmarine binocular, maker marked 'beh' for the manufactured Leitz. After the war Leitz became Leica who in turn destroyed all W.W.II. Leitz records. Even inquiries to the U.S. Government and Corning Glass proved unsuccessful so that determining the production history is apparently lost forever. You may ask, why Corning - After the war, the U.S. Government sent teams to Germany to retrieve all technical advancements that Germany had made during the war and to bring all the technology back to the U.S. for evaluation and to make use of anything of value. Corning got the optics advancements. This was likened to looting grandma's attic. You may recall that during the Carter administration, tons of W.W.II German material related to the manufacture of petroleum products from coal were pored over in an effort to find some economic solution to the "energy crises' of that period.

Common Markings, Terms and General Comments:

Mess Hall (Kantine) & Galley (Schiffskuche)
Teaspoon (Teeloffel), Tablespoon (Esloffel)
Serving Ladle (Schopfloffel)
Fork (Gabel), Desert Fork (Sussgabel)
Knife (Messer)
Table knife (Tischmesser) - two piece construction with
    nickel/ silver plated stainless steel blade and silver
    handle.

To transpose mm to inches, multiply by 0.0394. Thus
    210mm X 0.0394 = approximately 8 1/4 inches .

Although the swastika officially became the emblem for
    the Nazi Party on August, 7, 1920, at the Salzburg
    Congress; per USM Books, "There was absolutely
    no mandatory use of a swastika on silverware or
    silver service items that we are aware of."

The German Silver Makers Guild mandated that at
    least part of all cutlery sets carry the silver
    designation. This explains why some pieces of
    broken sets turn up with no designation.

RZM = Reichzeugmeisterei (National Equipment
    Quartermaster) founded in 1934 by the NSDAP as
    a Reich Hauptamt (State Central Office) The RZM
    procured and distributed items, approved designs,
    insured quality, supervised standardization and
    compliance to specifications.

RB = (Reichsbetrieb nummer) RB numbers replaced
    Manufacturer's names on products in 1942 to
    conceal the manufacturers name and therefore
    location from allied bombing.

Heer
> W.H. = Wehrmacht Heeres (Armed Forces Army)
> Army field, folding cutlery sets (Essbesteck) of
> either Knife/Spoon/Fork or Spoon/ Fork
> combinations are typically of aluminum for weight
> considerations

Kriegsmarine
> An "M" indicates Kriegsmarine and can appear
> either above or below the eagle
> The eagles can vary with simple 3 lined wings to 5
> full feathered wings as on C&CW produced items.

Luftwaffe
> Fl.U.V. = Flieger Unterkunft Verwaltung = Flight
>   Barracks Administration
> Eagles come in two variations: Early version with
> "Drooped Tail" on items marked up through 1941
> Later version with "Straight Tail" on items dated
> 1942 and later

SS

> SS-WVHA = SS-Wirtschafts und Verwaltungs
> Hauptamt (SS-Economic and Administration
> Department) - responsible for issuing personal
> equipment items
> SS-T.V. = SS-Totenkopfverbande
>   SS-Death's Head Units)
> SS-W.B. = SS-Wachverbande (SS-Guard Units)
> RZM/SS = SS items Quality controlled by RZM
>   1934 to 1943

NS = National Socialist

Photo Comment

Having made contact with several photographers as well as advertising at photography schools for assistance in the photography of the spoons - - all of which ended unsuccessful when informed of the number of photos required. As a result, I purchased a Canon A630, 8.0 Mega Pixel digital camera, tripods, lights, photo boxes etc., signed up for Apple's onetoone consulting and after taking hundreds of photos, have decided to go with these. At times I have used 'artistic license' by taking oblique photos where it was not possible to get a good straight on photo due to reflections etc. This sometimes makes the spoons appear to be non symmetrical and forks to look bottom heavy. I can assure you that German cutlery is symmetrical. The photo priority was to highlight the markings and not the piece per se. All photos were first edited with Apple's iPhoto '08 and then transferred to Apple's iWork's - Pages for final placement and adjustment. I still show up in one of the spoon bowels. Special thanks to Apple's Elizabeth for her patience and guidance, above and beyond the call of duty and to Alyssa for a clever way to move photos!

Special Note: Dated cutlery tends to disappear by 1943 as in 1942, total German losses KIA, WIA & MIA totaled 1.9 million, and 'advancing on all fronts' became a memory.

The post Nazi German Government's directions regarding 3rd Reich material: Relevant sections of German Law - summary of section § 86, 86a:

"Items that are used for making propaganda for a party or group which is classed as unconstitutional or forbidden, even if they act outside Germany, may not be spread inside Germany. This applies for items made to propagate ideas that correspond with the ideas of the "Third Reich". They might not be made, kept, imported or exported. The punishment may be prison (up to three years) or a fine.

This does not apply if those items are used in order to inform others, repel actions that are aimed against the constitution, if they are used in art, science, research, teaching, or to report about historical events or similar purposes.

If you use or show symbols or signs used by parties or groups that can be classified as unconstitutional, or if you manufacture, keep, export or import those, you may be punished (three years imprisonment or fine). You may not use or spread items that display or contain those signs or symbols, e.g. flags, insignia, uniforms (or parts of uniforms), mottos and forms of greeting. You may also not use or spread signs or symbols that look similar to those. This does not apply if those items are used in order to inform others, repel actions that are aimed against the constitution, if they are used in art, science, research, teaching, or to report about historical events or similar purposes."

Detailed Locations of Cutlery Photos and Text

Personal Service

PS-1 Adolf Hitler, Formal Pattern   26 & 27
PS-2 Adolf Hitler, Curved 'AH'   28 & 29
PS-3 Adolf Hitler, Ornamental   30 & 31
PS-4 Adolf Hitler, Raised ribs   32 & 33
PS-5 Eva Braun, Baroque   34 & 35
PS-6 Eva Braun, Parfait Spoon   36 & 37
PS-7 Herman Goering, Arms   38 & 39
PS-8 Herman Goering, Ribbed   40 & 41
PS-9 Herman Goering, RMarshall   42 & 43
PS-10 Heinrich Himmler, Train   44 & 45
PS-11 Heinrich Himmler   46 & 47
PS-12 Albert Speer   48 & 49
PS-13 Helmut Weidling   50 & 51
PS-14 Bernard Rust, DH   52 & 53
PS-15 Bernard Rust, DH   54 & 55
PS-16 Dr. Robert Ley, DAF   56 & 57
PS-17 Ernst Kaltenbrunner   58 & 59
PS-18 Fritz Sauckel   60 & 61
PS-19 Hans Frank   62 & 63
PS-20 Bishop Ludwig Mueller   64 & 65
PS-21 Martin Bormann   66 & 67
PS-22 Joachim von Ribbentrop   68 & 69
PS-23 Rudolf Hess   70 & 71
PS-24 Reinhard Heydrich   72 & 73

Note: The above sequence is based on acquisition date.

Other Government Cutlery

Wehrmacht Cutlery

SS Cutlery

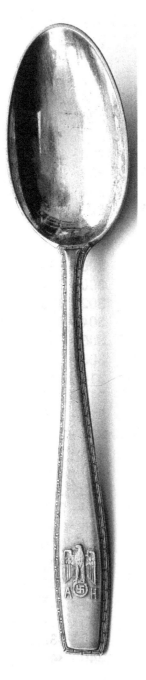

PS-1
L = 146 mm / 5 3/4"

PERSONALITY CUTLERY

PS-1   Hitler, Adolf "Formal Pattern"
(1889 - 1945)

Tea spoon.   Teeloffel: Obverse carries Hitler's personal eagle with static swastika straddled with A & H.. Reverse carries Reichsmark, 800 and Bruckmann eagle.

This is the most recognizable and available, likewise the most sought after of the Hitler memorabilia. As per Billy Price's, *Hitler, the Unknown Artist* "it is well known that the Fuhrer had personally designed these formal pieces featuring the "Fuhrer Adler" (the Leaders Eagle) with "A" and "H" to either side of the wreathed, static swastika in its talons." Much of Hitler's silver flatware was manufactured by the firm of P. Bruckmann & Sohne of Heilbronn an ancient town on the Neckar River in Wurttemberg. Bruckmann, (1805 - 1973), was one of the leading silver manufacturers in Germany. As a gift for Hitler's 50th birthday on 20 April 1939, Bruckmann presented some 3,000 pieces made up of six complete sets of 500 pieces, one set each for his 'Berghof' (Mountain Home), the Obersalzberg guest house and the 'Adlerhorst' (the Eagles Nest) nearby; the Nazi Party's 'Braune Haus' (Brown House) in Munich; his Prinzregertenplatz apartment in Munich and the 'Reichschancellery' Chancellery in Berlin. The tableware, needing to be harder and more durable, were made of .800 silver while the matching service pieces were made of .925 silver. The state formal pattern has a Greek Key "Meander" pattern, (representing the Greek river Meander as Hitler was an admirer of ancient Greece). Design assistance is sometimes attributed to Frau Professor and Architect Gerdy Troost (wife of Hitler's foremost architect - Paul Ludwig Troost) in any case, Hitler oversaw the effort.

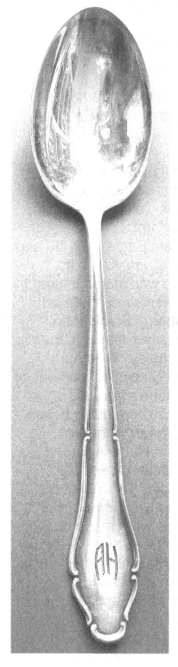

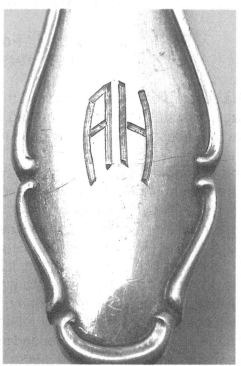

PS-2
L = 148 mm / 5 13/16"

PS-2   Hitler's, Curved AH monogram

Teaspoon. Obverse with curved AH monogram. Reverse
with 'Reichsmark' RM, 800 and the maker's mark of Lutz &
Weiss of Pforzheim, founded 1882. (a stylized L over W
inside a shield)

The curved monogram was also used on his crystal ware in
the Obersalzberg area.   Distinctive and unique to the
Berghof, Hitler's mountain retreat in the Alps per Mark D.
Griffith's *Liberated - Adolf Hitler Memorabilia*, published
1985, page 14. "The "AH" is side by side with outer edges
curved convex (outward). The top centers of the letters form
a peak in the middle and the bottoms of the letters are
proportionally indented. This spoon has the "flattop A" and is
executed in 4 strokes, one for the convex outer side, one for
the interior vertical, one for the top of the A and one for the
middle. The H is virtually a mirror image of the "A" without
the top stroke and is executed in three strokes."

Hitler Trivia: His uniforms are divided into 3 periods / styles:
1. Kampfzeit: The brown shirt with Sam Brown cross
    belt   1920's - 1933
2. Statesman: Fine brown tunic with white shirt   1933 -
    1939
3. Victory or Death: Field Gray tunic and white shirt
    1939 - 1945 (with SS sleeve eagle in Gold)

.

(Kampfzeit = Period of struggle)
or
(Der Kampfseit = The Struggle for Power)

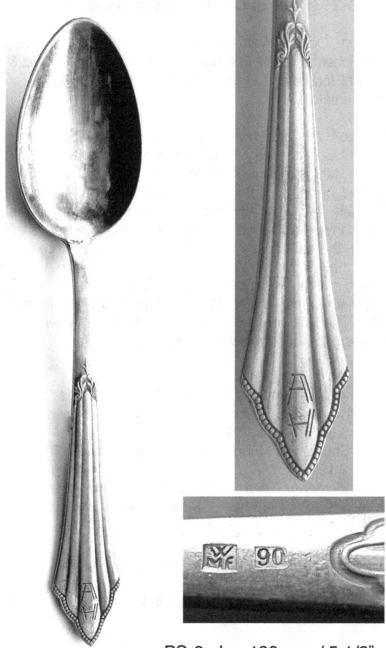

PS-3   L = 139 mm / 5 1/2"

PS-3   Hitler, Ornamented

Teaspoon. Obverse: Monogram: A over H, struck on the
center-wave of five from 1/ 2 of length, terminated with 41
dots patterned. Reverse. Hallmark: W over MF
(Wurttembergische Metallwarenfabrik, Geislingen 1853 to
the present) and 90

Note: Hitler's complimentary silver service pieces and
heavier items such as coffee & tea services, trays, coasters,
gravy boats, etc. typically came from August Wellner &
Sohne, of Aue (1854 - 1992) Germany's other leading silver
manufacturer.   Hitler's silverware patterns have the following
observed characteristics, in general: They are relatively
plain and utilitarian, symmetrical, well balanced, and display
very little - if any - ornamentation.

Fact: Hitler became a millionaire in 1931. On his 1933 tax
      return he declared an income of 1,232,335
      Reichmarks, subsequently he arranged to have himself
      exempted from taxes for life.   By 1944, some 12.5
      million copies of Mein Kampf had been printed with
      royalties to Hitler. He also collected royalties on the
      use of his likeness on postage stamps making him
      very wealthy. In 2000, his assets, still held by the
      Bavarian state were estimated to be worth $ 22 million.

Hitler trivia: His favorite part of the meal was desert. He
      relished cakes, pies and ice cream with strawberries
      drowned in mounds of whipped cream. He drowned his
      coffee and tea with sugar and cream. He favored
      Fachingen Heilwasser mineral water which is still
      available in Germany and is not to my taste!

PS-4
L = 134 mm / 5 1/4"

PS-4 Hitler, Alpaca*

Teaspoon. Obverse: Block A over H with triple raised ribs on
front, 3 pair of matched ribbons. Hallmark: Wellner with an
elephant over 'alpaca'.

> Although he was originally party member number 55,
> to make the party appear larger than it actually
> was, his membership number was registered as 555.
> Later after he had assumed control, he gave himself
> party number 7 to appear as a founder and mentioned
> same at the 1934 Nurnburg party meeting.

*Alpaca / Alpacca Silver - Also known in English as German
Silver or Nickel Silver and in french as maillechort is an alloy
composed of nickel, copper and zinc - contains NO silver.
The Alpacca alloy was created in 1823 by the German
chemist Dr. Ernst August Geitner (1783-1852). It is very
similar in its appearance to silver, but significantly cheaper.
Therefore, this new alloy was first called "Argentan". It
consisted of 20% nickel, 55% copper and 25% zinc. The new
silver-imitating alloy soon became very popular. The
Gebrueder Henninger (Henninger Bros.) proposed a similar
alloy (5-30% nickel, 45-70% copper and 8-45% zinc with
trace amounts of lead, tin and iron) which they called
"Neusilber". Later both Argentan and Neusilber were used
under the trade name of Alpacca (or Alpakka). The great
advantage of the use of Alpacca alloy as the base metal for
silver plating is that the appearance of the objects does not
change significantly with the wearing away of the silver layer.
Wellner's Alpaca formulation: Copper 65%, Zinc 23% and
Nickel 12%. (The elephant was a Wellner trademark.)

Trivia: The SS used Alpaca at many of its facilities and this
         service may have been a gift from the SS or used at
         SS functions.

PS-5
L = 142 mm / 5 10/16"

PS-5   Braun, Eva
(1912-1945)

Teaspoon. Obverse in a high relief, asymmetrical Baroque pattern, with the engraved 'EB' butterfly pattern monogram . Reverse carries the hallmark: 46 Jurst 50. The EB Butterfly monogram was designed by Albert Speer, perhaps her best friend and closest confidant at Obersalzberg.

In the 16 years of the Braun-Hitler relationship, Eva, spent the last ten years of her life virtually sequestered in the Berghof where Hitler provided everything for her. He even assigned her the monetary rights to some of his photos, taken by Hoffmann, which made her financially independent.

Two of her surviving quotes from 1945 - "I want to be a beautiful corpse" and after the wedding, "You may safely call me Frau Hitler."

She practiced Yoga

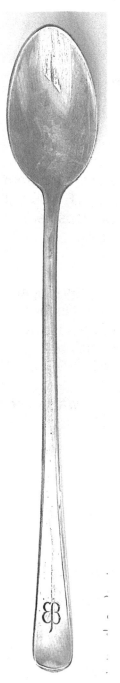

PS-6
L = 212 mm / 8 3/8"

PS-6   Braun, Eva

Iced Tea Spoon (Limonadeloffel), Obverse carries the **"EB"** butterfly monogram, A very plain symmetrical design with the single line engraved. Reverse carries unidentified maker mark: 'EKA' in block initials and '90 - 1 1/4' .

Per Albert Speer, "Eva Braun especially delighted in showing off her new patterns at any opportunity, frequently using a different pattern at each place of the table and asking her guests which patterns they preferred."

Braun Trivia: She was 23 years Hitler's junior and first met him when she was 17 in 1929.

38

PS-7
L = 137 mm / 5 7/8"

PS-7 Goering, Hermann
(1893-1946)

Teaspoon. Obverse with the Goering Coat-of-Arms, a right arm raised, facing right, grasping a ring. Pattern: Triple raised ribs, both sides, front and rear wheat pattern.
Reverse: 800, RM and the torch of Bremer Silberwarenfabrik 1905 - 1981 and KOPPEN. This Goring coat of arms logo is the 'un-ribbed' variant.

From Charles Hamilton's *"Leaders & Personalities of the Third Reich"* - Reich Marshal and Commander in Chief of the Luftwaffe, PrimeMinister of Prussia, Goering began his career as a fighter pilot in WWI and scored 22 kills, received the Pour le Merite, and was the last commander of Richthofen's squadron. In 1922 he joined the Nazi party and in 1923 was wounded in the unsuccessful Beer-Hall Putsch. After three years of exile in Sweden (Goering was later to talk Hitler out of invading this nation which gave him sanctuary), he returned to Germany and was one of the first Nazis elected to the Reichstag. On August 30 1932 he became president of the Reichstag.

He now focused on building up the Nazi police state, established the first concentration camps, and made Himmler chief of the Gestapo. By 1933, Goering was the second man in Germany and in 1935 was appointed by Hitler to command the Luftwaffe.

Luftwaffe failures in the Battle of Britain and the supply of Stalingrad cost Goering his standing with Hitler. He was semi retired for the last 2 years of the war. Tried at Nuremberg, found guilty - swallowed poison the morning of the execution 15Oct1946.

PS-8
L = 214 mm / 8 3/8"

PS-8 Goering Ribbed

Butter Knife: Obverse carries the Goering 'ribbed' Coat-of-Arms. Reverse 800, RM, HULSE.

Goering had literally dozens of sets of silver and thousands of individual pieces of Besteck (cutlery). He was given sets from France, England and numerous German districts. The Reichsmarschal did not favor Hitler's Wellner or Bruckmann but was partial to others such as Hulse. In the early years of Nazi power, Goering was the chief procurement officer of the military, the leader of the four-year plan, director of the 700,000 workers in the Goering Works and for all intents and purposes - a Head of State.

It was Goering who fined the German Jewish community a billion marks and ordered the elimination of Jews from the German economy, the 'Aryanization' of their property and businesses.

On Goering's 45th birthday - 12 Jan 1938, He accepted an exquisite Serves centerpiece from all the workers in his Four-Year Plan, who, at Goering's behest and most cheerfully he was sure, had received their last month's salaries deducted of 5% for the purchase of the gift.

Goering Trivia: He famously stated that, "I intend to plunder, and to do it thoroughly."
His IQ was 138!

Note: Butter knives are scarce as there is typically only one for every six place settings.

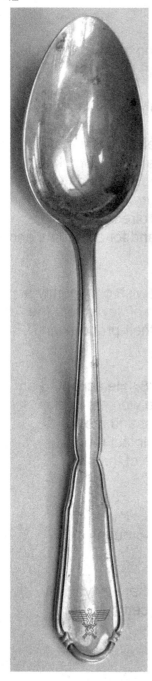

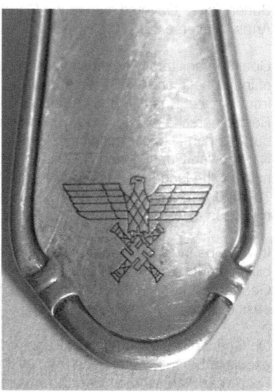

PS-9
L = 145 mm / 5 11/16"

PS-9 Goering RM

Teaspoon. The obverse carries his Reichsmarshall Coat of Arms, Pattern: recessed rib, both sides, full length of handle. Reverse: Reichsmark, 800 unidentified hallmark. This Monogram is the Type 3 Reichsmarschall Eagle

Goring Trivia - <u>As Reichminister of the Hunt</u> he outlawed: Horse-and-hound hunting, Shooting from cars, Claw and wire traps, Artificial lights to attract quarry and the issuance of hunting licenses to poor marksman. He Introduced American raccoons to Europe's forests.

As <u>Reich Forestry Minister:</u> Lighting cigarettes in a forest area was punishable by jail. Pushed scientific research to come up with a spray to do away with parasitic grubs. Passed special laws to protect endangered ferns, bushes and trees. Put irrigation schemes into effect. Had planted green recreational belts around industrial cities. Had 1,000 sq. miles of new trees planted from the Baltic to Austria. Created jobs for hundreds of thousands of unemployed building hutments and barracks, making roads, digging dikes, learning woodcraft and lumbering.

He favored a blue pencil for signing orders and documents,

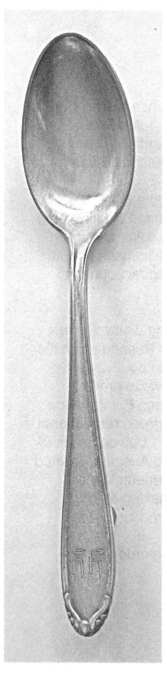

PS-10
L = 141 mm / 5 1/2"

PS-10 Himmler, Heinrich
(1900 - 1945)

Teaspoon. This pattern is known as his 'Train Pattern'.
Obverse with the runic **HH** Monogram in block letters.
Smooth art deco with raised rib, full length of handle.
Reverse: Hallmark: B (Bruckmann), a locomotive engine and
90 indicating heavy silver plate.

Reichsfuhrer-SS / RfSS, Head of the Gestapo and the
Waffen-SS and later Minister of Interior from 1943 to 1945.
After Hitler, the most powerful man in Nazi Germany during
1944 & 1945.

As a leading Nazis vegetarian, Himmler launched programs
to stop the SS from eating artificial honey, was against food
companies using refined flour and white sugar and banned
cigarettes in the Allgemeine-SS based on Nazi medical
research in the early 1930's linking both cigarettes and
asbestos to lung cancer. Interestingly, the Schwarzes Corps
sold tobacco during the kampfzeit period to raise money.

Trivia: Himmler's private trains: His Feldkommandostab
RfSS (Field HQ of the Rf-SS) was organized like a military
Hq and accompanied Himmler on his numerous tours. His
first, named "Sonderzug Heinrich" had fourteen carriages to
accommodate his staff, attached SS units including signals
section, escort battalion and flak detachment, reportedly, at
times up to 3,000 men accompanied the chief on his tours..
Later names were Steiermark and in 1944, temporarily
named Transport 44.

PS-11
L = 138 mm / 5 7/16"

PS-11 Himmler,

Teaspoon. Obverse with **HH,** a hand engraved script monogram of partially intertwined, vertical HH. Triple raised ribs on front only, Reverse with raised plain rib, unidentified hallmark: Ostrich (emu?) in diamond cartouche with a block 'WMF 18' (Wurttembergische Metallwarenfabrik, Geislingen founded in 1853 and still in operation).

Trivia - This failed chicken farmer actually received a diploma in agricultural chemistry from Munich Technical in 1922. His Nazi party number: 14,303. He joined the SS in 1925 with a membership number of 168. He held Blood Order #3.

During the 1930's, he is quoted. "I'm Party member number 2."

In 1934, Kurt Daluege, leader of SS-Gruppe Ost, refused to deal with "that Bavarian chicken breeder Himmler."

Himmler favored a green pencil for signing orders and documents, green ink being a prerogative of government ministers.

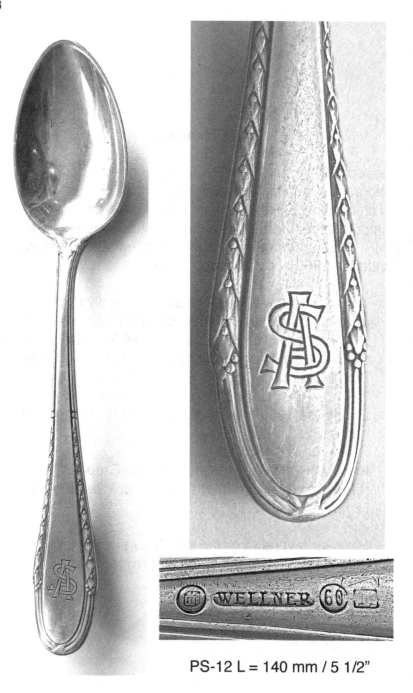

PS-12 L = 140 mm / 5 1/2"

49

PS-12 Speer, Albert
(1905 - 1981)

Teaspoon.   Obverse with intertwined 'AS': Reverse:
Hallmark: Wellner logo, 'WELLNER' '60' in a circle and
unreadable style number in a square.. He personally
designed the monogram of the Intertwined, block AS

As Hitler's architect he designed and supervised the
construction of both the new Reich Chancellery in Berlin
(arguably the most profound statement of 'NAZI" architecture
and referred to as the most beautiful building ever
constructed) and the Party palace in Nuremberg. Reich
Minister for Armaments and War Production from February
1942 to 1945. On 1 November 1944, Speer instituted the
Notprogramm (emergency program) virtually halting all
aircraft manufacture except that of jets and single engine
fighters. He reorganized war production and in spite of
massive allied bombing attacks raised the 1941 production
of front-line machines of 9,540 and heavy tanks of 2,900 to
35,350 front-line machines and 17,300 tanks, as well as
raising overall fighter aircraft production to 3,000 a month in
1944 with FW-190's reaching 1,000 per month with some
20,000+ having been produced. Over 30,000 ME-109's
were produced. Speer's efforts probably prolonging the war
by at least 2 years. His NAZI party number was 474,481
and his IQ was 128.

He favored a red pencil for signing orders and documents,

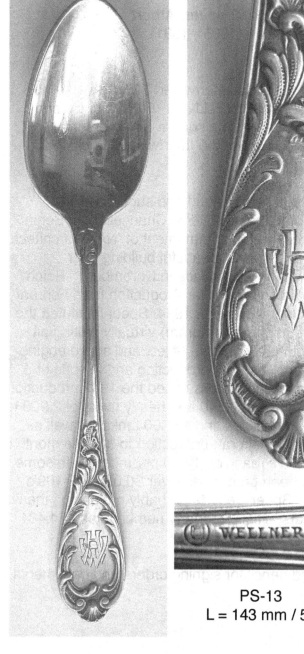

PS-13
L = 143 mm / 5 5/8"

PS-13 Weiding, Helmut (1891 - 1955)
(General of the Artillery - 2nd highest regular Army rank)

Teaspoon. The obverse carries his personal pattern of **'HW'**. The **HW** monogram has the letters intertwined and outlined in block style. Reverse maker marked: 'die - 4 & 2 showing, '"Wellner" and plating mark of '90' and a style number of '21'

In 1944 he was awarded the Knights Cross with Oak Leaves and Swords. In 1945, he was appointed defense commandant of Berlin and the General in Command of the LXI Panzer Group. The Soviet forces under Marshall Zukhov had 2,500,000 troops, 6,000 tanks and 40,000 artillery pieces facing 300,000 men, many of them Hitler Youth down to the age of 12! The Soviets lost 400,000+ vs 300,000 German civilian and military casualties. He surrendered Berlin on 2 May 1945, was captured by the Soviets, condemned to 25 years in prison and died in Russian captivity in 1955.

During the April 1945 defense of Berlin, he is quoted regarding the use of Hitler Youth, "You cannot sacrifice these children for a cause that is already lost."

PS-14T
L = 210 mm / 8 1/4"

PS-14 Rust, Bernard's
(1883-1945)

Tablespoon & Demitasse spoon. **'Dh'** for Deutsche-
Hochschule, short-form for German Higher Education. This
is his Ministry's official state pattern. Table spoon has an
unmarked obverse while the "DH" below the national eagle
appears on the reverse of the spoon. Maker Marked: BR
(acia). HENNEBERG BM, a scale in a circle followed by '90'
in a square.

Prior to WWI, he was a senior master at a secondary school.
A WWI Lieutenant, he suffered a serious head wound,
receiving the Iron Cross 1st class. During April 1934 he was
appointed Reich Minister of Science, Education and Popular
Culture till 1945. Purged all Jews from the universities.
Dismissed over 1,000 professors including a number of
Nobel Prize winners thus hindering German science studies.
Rust reported that he had "liquidated the school as an
institution of intellectual acrobatics." Committed suicide on 8
May 1945 by gunshot.

PS-15D
L = 109 mm / 4 5/16"

PS-15 cont. Rust, Bernard

Small silver demitasse spoon (Moccaloffel) marked **"Dh"** below the national eagle on the obverse. Dh for "Deutsche-Hochschule" or German Higher Education, his official state pattern. Maker Marked on the reverse: 'Br Henneberg BM' a scale in a circle, and '90' in a square.

Among the Nobel prize winners he had dismissed were Albert Einstein, James Franck, Fritz Haber, Otto Warburg and Otto Meyerhof. His comment, "We must have a new Aryan generation at the universities, or else we will lose the future."

Note: One dealer ascribed the 'Dh' monogram to the Deutscher Hof Hotel although most hotels mark their full name on their cutlery as is the Deutscher Hof butter knife in Miscellaneous M-137.

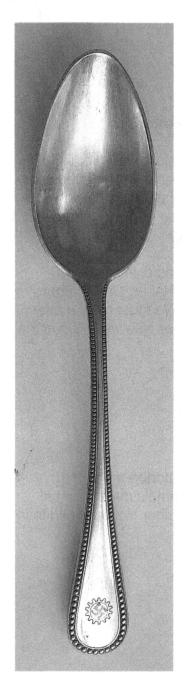

PS-16
L = 216 mm / 8 1/2"

PS-16 Ley, Dr. Robert
(1890-1945)

Tablespoon. 'DAF' for Deutsche Arbeitsfront - German Labour Front; Tablespoon owned by DAF leader Dr. Robert Ley and carries his Ministry's official state pattern on the obverse. Other patterns: Beaded ribs. both sides, front and back, the length of the handle. Maker marked: a Die in a circle, "WELLNER", "90" in a circle, "45" in a square. By far, much more rare than Hitler's flatware pieces.

With the 10 May 1933 founding of DAF, through the 'coordination' (gleichschaltung) of all trade unions, DAF with 25 Million members was composed of all trade unions, corporate and professional associations and might better be translated as "Work Force" since the organization included both employers and employees. This accomplished Hitler's direction for "all who create with head and hand" to be under a single Nazi controller. He also headed the Kraft Durch Freude - 'Strength through Joy' & the Volkswagen factory (no VW's were ever delivered). The DAF emblem was a cogged wheel (Zahnrad) with 14 teeth encompassing a mobile swastika. Dr. Ley commented on the trade unions, "Ideologically speaking, the class war was anchored in the trade unions. and the trade unions lived off this." Dr. Ley committed suicide on 24 October 1945.

Note: A sub organization of DAF, the SdA - Schonheit der Arbeit (Beauty of Labor) which was established in 1934 and headed by Albert Speer, supplied canteens with flatware and cutlery. Initial production was of minimal quality reflecting the general poor economic conditions. The Farben spoon OG-37 exhibits the early period. Later cutlery exhibit better material and much better appearance.

Nicknamed: "Reich Drunk Master."

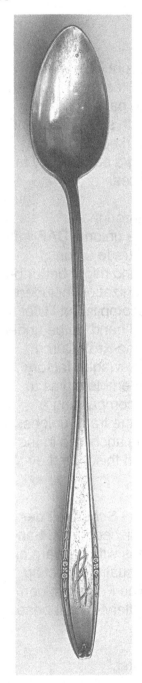

PS-17
L = 224 mm / 8 13/16"

PS-17 Kaltenbrunner, Dr. Ernst
(1903-1946)

Ice tea / parfait spoon. The obverse carries his personal 'EK' monogram, double lined with highlights between. Front and back symmetrical with 3 flowers straddling the initials. Maker marked: 'AWS' in a square box (August Wellner & Sohne), an elephant, '100' silver plate in a circle and '24' style number in a square box. The AWS maker mark was used by Wellner from 1928 to 1938.

A lawyer and fanatical Austrian Nazi with an IQ of 113, he along with Seyes-Inquart (IQ 141) were the leaders of the Austrian SS from 1934, prior to Anschluss in 1938. In January 1943 he became the 2nd and last Chief of the Reich Main Security Office, (RSHA) succeeding Heydrich with a rank of SS-Obergruppenfuhrer, equivalent to a U.S. Army rank of Lt. General (3 stars). Under his tireless direction, the RSHA was responsible for hunting down and exterminating several million civilians, primarily Jews in the East. Hanged in Nuremberg on 16 October 1946.

Nicknamed "The Callous Ox". NAZI party number 300,179

PS-18
L = 213 mm / 8 7/16"

PS-18 Sauckel, Fritz
(1984-1946)

Tablespoon, obverse carries his State pattern of the 'Thuringian Eagle', with its broken wing. Maker marked: "Bruckmann 90" on the reverse.

As the General Plenipotentiary for the Distribution of Labour (Generalbevollmächtigter für den Arbeitseinsatz), 1942 - 1945 he was responsible for directing the deportation of some 5 million slave laborers from the occupied territories, primarily Poland, Ukraine and other eastern countries, to work in German war related industries. With an IQ of 118, he rose from Thuringia's district manager in 1925 to Governor in 1933. He was also both an honorary SA and SS General. At Nuremberg he was "shocked in his innermost soul" to find out about the Nazi atrocities. His most remembered defense, "just following orders".

Trivia: Sauckel's workers quotas were set by Albert Speer. Speer's labor shortage was primarily due to the prohibition on using German women in industrial jobs. During the Nuremberg trial in 1946 Sauckel pointed at Albert Speer and said, "There is a man you should hang." Speer was sentenced to 20 years. Sauckel was hanged on 16 Oct 1946.

PS-19
L = 217 mm / 8 9/16"

63

PS-19 Frank, Dr. Hans
(1900 - 1946)

Tablespoon, The obverse carries his machine incised, official state pattern of the Governor General of Poland. Maker marked on the reverse with: '45' in a square, '90' in a circle, "ART. KRUPP", their trademark 'Bear with 'ART KRUPP' over and "BERNDORF" under" followed by 'BERNDORF'.

With an IQ of 130, he was the Nazi Party's leading jurist and Governor General of Poland. Prior to 1933, as Hitler's lawyer, he successfully defended Hitler in several hundred actions and afterwards become Reich Minister of Justice. Out of favor with Hitler, he was sent to Poland in 1939 as punishment, where he earned the unofficial title of 'Slayer of Poles'. Hitler's direction to Frank, "The task which I give you is a devilish one, other people to who territories are entrusted would ask, 'What will you construct?' I shall ask the opposite." In October 1939 Frank said, "The Poles shall be the slaves of the German Reich." and in 1944, "I have not hesitated to declare that when a German is shot, up to 100 Poles shall be shot too." Hanged as a war criminal in Nuremberg 16 Oct 1946.

Note: Identical tableware has been represented (by the same dealer as had commented on the Rust's spoon) as from the 'Castle Klessheim' located near Salzburg, Austria, a luxurious government guest residence maintained to house dignitaries waiting to see Hitler at the Burghof. This was vigorously denied by my source.

PS-20
L = 218 mm / 8 9'16"

PS-20   Bishop Ludwig Mueller
(1883 -1945)

Tablespoon: The obverse carries the Deutsche Christen symbol of a Christian cross with a mobile swastika in the middle encompassed by a shield. Reverse maker marked Koch & Bergfeld of Bremen, (founded 1829), 800, and RM. From Bishop Ludwig Mueller's service.

In 1932 the Protestant church came under the influence of a Nazi movement called "German Christians", (also called "Stormtroopers of Jesus"). The Deutsche Christen (DC) became the voice of Nazi ideology within the Evangelical Church and approved by Hitler, they proposed a church "Aryan paragraph" to prevent "non-Aryans" from becoming ministers or religious teachers. Only a very few Christians opposed Nazism such as the "Confessing Christians". The German Christian Movement was strongly nationalistic and adopted Luther's anti Semitism (ref his 1543 book, "On Jews and Their Lies") as well as his respect for authority (see Romans 13). Composed of the radical wing of German Lutheranism, the main Protestant branch supported the Nazi ideology, reconciling Christian doctrine with German nationalism and anti semitism. This movement represented Hitler's "Positive Christianity" views as lawfully encoded into the Nazi "constitution."

In the 1933 church elections, Hitler made a radio appeal in support of the German Christian movement and later appointed Ludwig Mueller, Reich Bishop of the Protestant Church. Bishop Mueller committed suicide in 1945!

Fact: In 1925, of the German population of 65 million, some 40 million were Evangelical Lutherans and 21 million Roman Catholics.

PS-21
L = 112 mm / 4 7/16"

PS-21 Martin Bormann
(1900 - 1945)

Egg spoon: Carries the 'Bormann Eagle on the obverse.
Reverse carries 'Aluminium-Germany'.   Dealer states: "the
Martin Bormann egg spoon came directly from Bormann's
house wreckage at the Obersalzberg! a very rare and
extremely difficult to locate pattern."

Born in 1900 he joined the party in 1927 and became chief
of staff for Rudolf Hess. Made head of the Party chancellery
in 1941 and Hitler's personal secretary in April 1943. He was
a major advocate of Gleichschaltung (coordination). This
was the umbrella term under which virtually all major civilian
organizations in the political, economic and social life of the
German nation were placed under Nazi control   By the end
of WWII he had become second only to Hitler in terms of real
political power and an SS General to boot. Bormann was
killed on 2 May 1945 while attempting to escape Berlin after
Hitler's suicide. At Nuremberg in 1946, due to lack of
information regarding his death, he was tried as a war
criminal and sentenced to death in absentia.

Party # 60,508 acquired after his rise to power and qualified
him for a Golden Party Badge

A second opinion identified the spoon as a typical souvenir
(Andenkens) offered at the prewar, annual NSDAP
Nuremberg rally (Reichsparteitag) held in early September
and focused on strengthening Hitler's position as Germany's
savior. This spoon has no characteristics of andenkens as
exhibited by real andenkens M-148 & M-149.

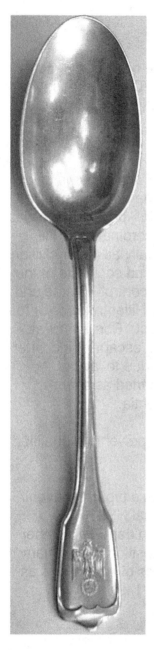

PS-22
L = 208 mm / 8 2/16"

PS-22 Joachim von Ribbentrop
(1893-1946)

Tablespoon: The obverse features a raised Reich eagle and swastika, the same type as used on the formal pattern AH flatware but with subtle differences in the Eagle and without the AH monogram. The reverse marked "RM, 925 and dot inside circle" (possibly a variation Bruckmann mark). The 925 (sterling silver) is unusual for cutlery.

As Hitler's Minister of Foreign Affairs (1938-1945), IQ of 129 this pristine flatware piece may have been used by Hitler and by von Ribbentrop as a special setting for the highest Foreign Ministry / Diplomatic dinners or functions.

A truly controversial personality. Wounded and winner of the Iron Cross 1st Class in WWI. Married Anneliese Henkel, daughter of the largest German champagne manufacturer. Joined the Party on 1 May 1932, member 1,119,927 and Winner? of the Nazi Golden Party Badge. Ambassador to England 1936-1938. Negotiated the treaty with Russia. On 11 August 1939 Ribbentrop stated, "We want war." He was blamed for convincing Hitler that Britain would not react to an attack on Poland and thus starting WWII. In August 1939, Goring said, "Now you've got your @%#* war. It's all your doing!" In 1943 Hitler said, "He is greater than Bismarck". The other prominent members of Hitler's inner circle saw him as arrogant, vain, touchy, humorless and contemptible for his haughty incompetence. Goering referred to him publicly as that "dirty little champagne pedlar", Goebbels remarked: "He bought his name, he married his money and he swindled his way into office". He testified at Nuremberg: "Do any of us look like murderers" and "There are lots of things I did not know" he was tried, convicted and hung at Nuremberg,

Nicknames: "Ribbensnob", "Iago

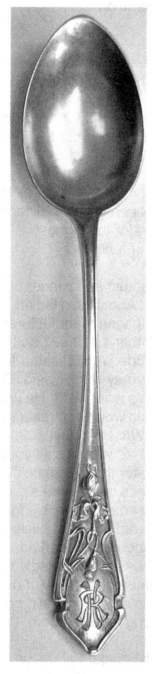

PS-23   L = 112 mm / 4 6/16"

PS-23   Rudolf Hess
(1894 - 1987)

Demitasse spoon: Obverse bears the Rudolf Hess "R.H." monogram in art nouveau pattern. The reverse bears 800 RM, and the most likely maker's mark of Vereinigte Silberwarenfabriken of Dusseldorf.

Hess joined the party in 1920, wrote Mein Kampf as dictated by Hitler where he was able to introduce his own ideas regarding *lebensraum.* As Deputy Leader of the Nazi Party, in 1939 he became the No. 3 man in Nazi Germany when he was made successor designate to Hitler and Goering. He embarked on a self-appointed secret peace mission to Britain on 10 May 1941 and was imprisoned and treated as a prisoner of war. Sentenced to life imprisonment at Nuremberg. He died, the only inmate in Spandau prison, on 17 Aug 1987. His son quotes his father's statement uttered at the Nuremberg trial: "I regret nothing!"   IQ 120 est

Hess, the man, had a strong interest in astrology, the occult. and a deep interest in herbal and homeopathic medicine, as well as organic gardening and biodynamic agriculture. Hess was a vegetarian who strongly advocated animal welfare. He oversaw recycling programs and was an ardent conservationist. Hess ordered a mapping of all the ley lines in the Third Reich which defined the Externsteine rock formation in Lower Saxony as the center of Germany.

Dealer states that the piece came from Sergeant Richard Cowling, the GI looter who stole the silverware from the Hess estate at Reicholdsgrün in lower Bavaria. This is supported by a sworn statement from Phyllis Orsi dating from July 2, 2005, where she certifies before a Michigan notary public as to the authenticity of the item.

Nicknamed: The Brown Mouse"

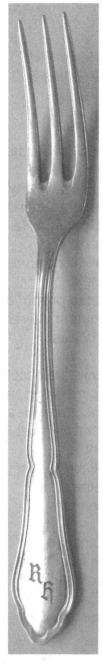

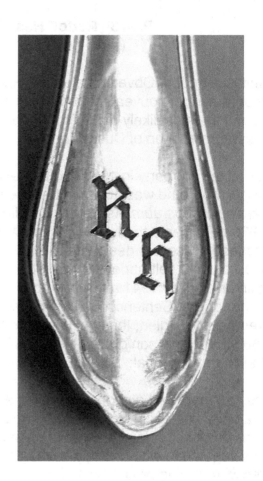

PS-24
L = 144 mm / 5 11/16"

PS-24 Reinhard Heydrich
(1902 - 1942)

Cocktail Fork: The obverse carries his personal, hand engraved, monogram of a staggered 'RH'. Reverse: Wellner die, WELLNER 100 in a circle and 18 in a square.

Tall, slim, blond with blue eyes, a first class fencer, excellent horseman, pilot and violin player (he joined Mrs. Himmler in duets) he was the epitome of the Nordic-Aryan type. Became Commander of the Security Police, the Security Service (SD) and Gestapo. Joined the SS in 1931, became a Major in December, a Colonel in July 1932, Brig General March 1933. As Heinrich Himmler's number two he secured control of the Munich and Bavarian police in 1933. For his role in "The Night of the Long Knives' he became a Lt. General in July 1934. In 1936 he directed the forging of documents that convinced Stalin that his 35,000 man officer corp was plotting against him resulting in Stalin obliterating half of the corps. In 1939 he provided Hitler with the justification for the invasion of Poland. Focused on the Jewish question, in 1941 he stated, " the Fuhrer has ordered the physical extermination of the Jews." The code word for the extermination of Polish Jewry was 'Operation Reinhard'. In September 1941 he moved to Prague as Deputy Reich Protector of Bohemia and Moravia.   Personally convened the Wannsee Conference on 20 Jan 1942 to effect the "Final Solution". On 27 May 1942 he was wounded by Free Czech agents and died on 4 June 1942. In reprisal, the German's killed some 15,000 Czechs.

Nicknames: The Blond Beast, The Butcher

Note: Regarding the forks provenance: Dealer states, "It came back from WWII with a 506th PIR 101st A/B officer"

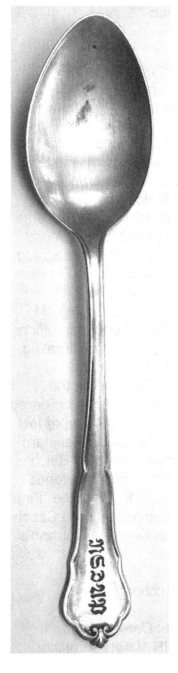

OG-25
L = 133 mm / 5 1/4"

OTHER GOVERNMENT

OG-25 'NSDAP'.
Nationalsozialistische Deutsche Arbeiterpartei

Teaspoon. Spoon carries NSDAP in Fraktur print on the obverse. Maker marked on reverse: RM, '800' and 'HTB' for Hanseatishe Silberwarenfabrik, Bremen.

National Socialist German Workers Party: Founded in 1919 as the German Workers Party (DAP), the name was changed to NSDAP in 1920 to broaden its appeal.

Fraktur Trivia: The first FRAKTUR typeface was designed when Holy Roman Emperor Maximilian (1493-1519) had the new type (German Script) created. It remained popular in Germany into the early 20th Century. On 3 January 1941, Martin Bormann issued a circular letter to all public offices which declared FRAKTUR (and its corollary, the Sutterlin based hand writing) to be Judenlettern (Jewish letters) and prohibited its further use and replacing it with 'antiqua'. ie the spoon predates 3Jan41.

A second explanation from Maik Kopleck's *BERLIN 1933-1945*, "its use was forbidden by a decree issued by Bormann on Hitler's order because in the annexed territories it had led to confusion."

Surprisingly, the letterhead of Bormann's decree was in Fraktur type!

The waste of manpower, material and paper in replacing all school books, street signs, typewriter keys etc. in war time was monumental.

OG-26
L = 141 mm / 5 9/16"

OG-26 NSDAP'

Teaspoon. High Leader's spoon, The obverse carries a
Swastika surrounded by oak leaves - (Eichenlaub or EL), a
symbol of strength. End is squared. Maker marked on the
reverse: RM, 800 GR for Gebruder Reiner, Krumbach
Bayern. Founded 1914,

Under the NSDAP, the National Colors (Reichsfarben) were
Black, White and Red. The early NSDAP slogan:
Deutschland Erwache - Germany Awake.

NSDAP Promise of Loyalty - I promise loyalty to my
Fuhrer Adolf Hitler. I promise to always meet him and
the leaders he will determine for me with respect
and obedience.

Symbolism of: Oak Leaves = Spirited Struggle
Palm Leaves = Victory

OG-27
L = 211 mm / 8 1/4"

OG-27 NSDAP/SA

Tablespoon. This aluminum tablespoon's eagle is looking to its left shoulder which symbolizes the Nazi party and was called the Parteiadler. In the absence of any specific organizational emblem, it is appropriate to assign it to either the NSDAP or the SA. Unidentified maker mark "C&C.W. 40".

In 1929, Hitler described the SA man as, "The SA attracts the militant natures among the Germanic breed, the men who think democratically, unified by a common allegiance."

80

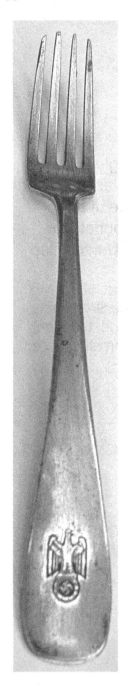

OG-28
L = 210 mm / 8 1/4"

OG-28 NSDAP/SA

Dinner Fork: The Obverse carries a very early eagle with down swept wings. A representation typical of an early service used by a political leader. The reverse is maker marked 'GEBR.HEPP and '90'. This fork has the eagle looking to his left shoulder symbolizing the Nazi party. Again, in the absence of any specific organizational logo, it is appropriate to assign it to either the NSDAP or the SA.

Gebruder Hepp located in Pforzheim, Germany since 1863 was acquired by WMF (Wuerttemberg Metalware Factory) in 1988 and is noted for making many of the silver service items for the larger German hotels.

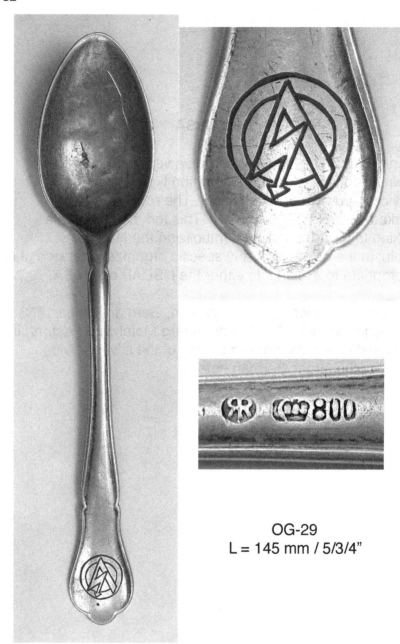

OG-29
L = 145 mm / 5/3/4"

OG-29 'SA'

Teaspoon. The spoon carries the stylized pseudo-runic "SA" monogram on the obverse. Maker mark: reversed "R" facing 'R' of Rossdeutscher & Reisig of Breslau, with RM, 800'.

The Sturmabteilung abbreviated SA, (German for "Assault detachment" or "Assault section", usually translated as "stormtroop(er)s"), It played a key role in Adolf Hitler's rise to power in the 1930s.

SA men were often called "brown shirts", for the color of their uniforms, and to distinguish them from the Schutzstaffel (SS), who wore black and brown uniforms (compare the Italian black shirts). Brown colored shirts were chosen as the SA uniform because a large batch of them were cheaply available after World War I, having originally been ordered for German troops serving in Africa.

In 1930, to ensure the loyalty of the SA to himself, Adolf Hitler assumed command of the entire organization and remained Oberster SA-Führer for the remainder of the group's existence to 1945. The day to day running of the SA was conducted by the Stabschef SA (SA Chief of Staff). After 1931, it was the Stabschef who was generally accepted as the Commander of the SA, acting in Hitler's name.

Favorite sayings: "Terror must be broken by terror", and
    "All opposition must be stamped into the ground"

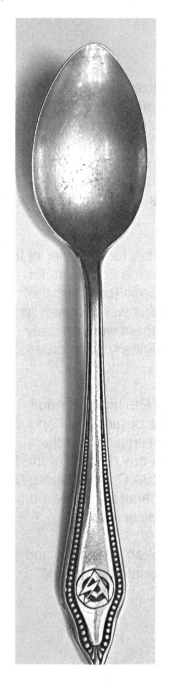

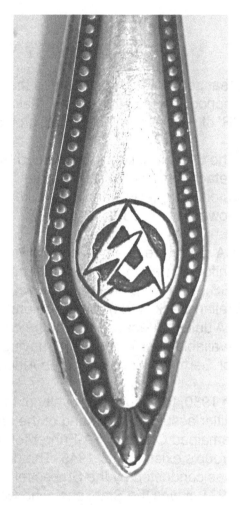

OG-30
L = 143 mm / 5 5/8"

OG-30 'SA'

Teaspoon. The spoon carries the stylized "SA" monogram on the obverse. Reverse marked with RM, '800'. Maker mark 'JRN' not identified

Sturmabteilung (German for "Storm Department", usually translated as "stormtroop(er)s")   The SA was the first paramilitary organization of the NSDAP - the German Nazi party. These were the "brown shirts". From its inception in 1921 till its demise in 1945, there were less than 200 men that occupied the top three positions in the SA. At its height in August 1934 there were some 2.9 million members. The SA was also the first Nazi paramilitary group to develop pseudo-military titles for bestowal upon its members. The SA ranks would be adopted by several other Nazi Party groups, chief among them the SS. The SA was very important to Hitler's rise to power until they were superseded by the SS after the 'Night of the Long Knives' of 30 June 1934 when the leadership of the SA were purged.

The SA motto: Alles Fur Deutschland - Everything for Germany was also the motto of the NSKK.

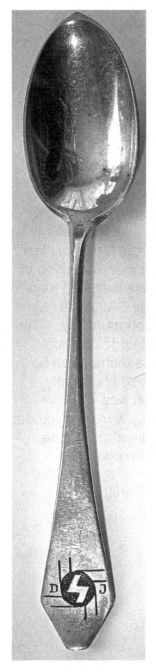

OG-31
L = 135 mm / 5 5/16"

OG-31   DJV Deutsche Jungvolk (German Youth)

Teaspoon. The obverse carries the sigrune in the center straddled by the 'D' and the 'J' over a stylized swastika. On the reverse: 'O.R.G.M' RM 800 'F' in a circle (Friedrich Feuerstein, Hanau).

In July 1926, the Hitler-Jugend, Bund Deutscher Arbeiterjugend (Hitler Youth, League of German Worker Youth) became an integral part of the Sturmabteilung. By 1929, the Hitler-Jugend had enlisted over 25,000 boys aged 14 and upwards. It also set up a junior branch, the Deutsches Jungvolk (DJV) for boys aged 10 to 14.

The sigrune emblem first became associated with the DJV on 9 November 1929 on the 6th anniversary of the failed Beer Hall Putsch when their first official flag consisting of a black field with a central silver sigrune was presented. The sigrune was adopted as the official emblem of the DJV and was used on assorted insignia but the design was unusual as even the early youth memorabilia usually only featured the more conventional Nazi swastika.

Jungvolk Oath (taken by ten-year-old boys on first entering the DJV)

"In the presence of this blood banner which represents our Führer, I swear to devote all my energies and my strength to the savior of our country, Adolf Hitler. I am willing and ready to give up my life for him, so help me God."

OG-32
L = 132 mm / 5 3/16"

89

OG-32 'HJ', Hitler-Jugend

Teaspoon. Obverse carries the HJ Logo. Reverse marked RM 800.

The HJ existed from 1922 to 1945, the 2nd oldest paramilitary NAZI group founded one year after the Sturmabteilung (SA) and attached to the SA. In July 1926 The Hitler-Jugend Bund der Deutschen Arbeiterjugend (Hitler Youth, League of German Worker Youth) received its final name. The HJ was banned in April 1932 by Chancellor Bruning but Chancellor von Papen lifted that ban in June 1932. The HJ diamond was adopted as the organizations emblem in 1933 along with its colors of Red and Black.. Membership became compulsory in December 1936. By 1945, the Volksturm commonly drafted 12 year old HJ members into its ranks for the defense of the fatherland. HJ motto: "Blut Und Ehre - Blood and Honor. Notable slogans: "Live Faithfully, Fight Bravely, and Die Laughing!" and "We were born to die for Germany!"

Hitler Youth Oath - In the presence of this blood banner which represents our Fuhrer, I swear to devote all my energies and my strength to the savior of our country, Adolf Hitler, I am willing and ready to give up my life for him, so help me God.

HJ Trivia: During the Battle of Berlin, The Reich Youth Leader (Reichsjugenfuhrer), Artur Axmann formed the HJ into a major part of the defense commencing at the Seelow Heights. General Weidling ordered Axmann to disband the HJ combat formations but in all the confusion his order was never carried out.

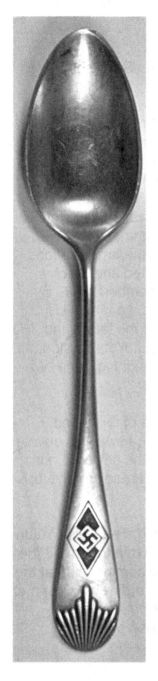

OG-33
148 mm / 5 13/**16**"

OG-33 Hitlerjugend (Hitler Youth)

Teaspoon, Obverse with the HJ symbol. Reverse marked RM, 800, unidentified maker's mark

As early as 1922, the NAZI youth organization, Jungeturm Adolf Hitler was formed. At the 4 July 1926 Reichsparteitag (National Party day) meeting in Nurnberg, the name Hitler Jungend (Hitler Youth) was announced. In 1933 at age 26, Balder von Schrach became Reich Youth Leader (1933 - 1940) head of the HJ. In 1936 at age 29 he achieved the SA rank of Gruppenfuhrer (2 star General) and also became a State Secretary and later Governor of Vienna (1940 - 1945). Interestingly, two of Schrach's ancestors were signatories of our Declaration of Independence and his father in law, Heinrich Hoffmann, supplied the photos for his books which focused on NAZI ideas of character, discipline, obedience and leadership as described in his best selling Die Hitler-Jugend (1934).

At age 10, boys joined the Deutsches Jungvolk (German Young People), at age 13 they transferred into the Hitler Jugend until age 18. The HJ became compulsory in 1936 which drove membership to 8.8 million. This was the venue for the para-military training of a generation of soldiers. Girls from ten to eighteen were given their own parallel organization, the Bund Deutscher Mädel (BDM), League of German Girls. Hitler's goal for the HJ, "The weak must be chiseled away. I want young men and women who suffer pain. A young German must be as swift as a greyhound, as tough as leather and as hard as Krupp's steel."

Per Schrach, 'Loyalty is everything and everything is the love of Adolf Hitler."

OG-34
L = 213 mm / 8 6/16

OG-34 HJ/RFS

Hitler Youth "Reichsfuhrerschule der HJ (National-Leaders-School of the HJ)

Tablespoon. The obverse is stamped with the Hitler Youth diamond and swastika, beneath which is similarly impressed "RFS" for 'Reichsfuhrerschule" (National-leaders-school). The reverse is jeweler engraved "Mehlem" and maker marked with "Hanseat" the manufacturer's name, followed by the silver plate of "90".

Under the direct control of Reichsjugendfuhrer Balder von Schirach, the RFS were to train HJ leaders. Mehlem being the location of one of the three HJ National Leaders Schools - this one near Bonn, the others in Potsdam and for women, in Godesberg. Upon successful completion of the training, graduates were authorized to wear a special insigne over the right breast tunic pocket. This insigne consisted of a silver embroidered bar of oak leaves with the initials, "RFS" outlined in black surmounting the oak leaves.

In addition to the traditional German school system, and the HJ special training, the Nazis established elite schools for the training of the young Nazis: the exclusive Ordensburgen (Order Castles) took the top graduates from earlier schooling and at a nominal age of 18 they were trained for another three years to be ready to assume high level positions in the Nazi Party. An example would be the Ordenberg Vogelsang where the original building has been preserved at this new national park and although designed to appear as a medieval castle, its NS architecture is easily recognizable. Most of the original grandiose statuary remains but with the obvious NS markings removed. Construction on this hugh complex was started in 1936!

94

OG-35
L = 212 mm / 8 6/16"

OG-35 HJ Sportschule Braunau

Soupspoon: Obverse carries the HJ emblem over 'Sportschule, Braunau'. Reverse has unknown maker mark of 'EMD' with 90.

The HJ put more emphasis on physical and military training than on academic study.

In 1935, about 60 percent of Germany's young people belonged to the HJ.   With the annexation of both Austria and Czechoslovakia in March of 1938, the various German created youth organizations (HJ, DJV, BDM & DJM) added over 1 million to their numbers and by 1939, about 82 percent (7.3 million) of eligible youths within the Greater Reich belonged making it the largest youth organization in the world. 1939 was declared "The Year of Physical Training" and introduced the Sports Competition. Medals were awarded to youths who performed rigorous athletic drills and met strict physical fitness standards. Every summer, a day would now be set aside as the "Day of the State Youth" for these events. School schedules were adjusted to allow for at least one hour of physical training in the morning and one hour each evening. Prior to this, only two hours per week had been set aside. Hitler also encouraged young boys to take up boxing to heighten their aggressiveness.

> Note: this training center (Sportschule / Physical Training Academy) for selected HJ athletes was located in the town of Hitler's birth, Braunau, Austria. After the 13 March 1938 annexation, Hitler made his first entry into Austria at Braunau

OG-36
L = 210 mm / 8 1/4"

OG-36 DAF / SdA
(Schonheit der Arbeit / Beauty of Work)

Tablespoon: The obverse has a raised central spine and is unmarked. Reverse carries the logo of the 'Modell Des Amtes/Schonheit der Arbeit' (Model of the Office/Beauty of Work) with the DAF cogwheel, a maker mark of HLM and "Rustfrei "

Within the DAF, was the Kraft durch Freude - KdF (Strength through Joy) and within the KdF was Amt für Schönheit der Arbeit. The SdA, Schonheit dr Arbeit" (Beauty of Labor) organization was established as a subsection of the KdF under the control of Albert Speer (from 1933 to at least 1936) who was responsible for improving working conditions in factories, including setting up canteens and supplying the cutlery.

The SdA goal was described in Shelley Barunowski's "*Strength Through Joy*" as "Aestheticizing the shop floor meant eliminating class conflict and creating the plant community, as well as reconstructing the identities of workers so that they would become full-fledged members of the racial community."

The Governments focus was to create practical workplace benefits while simultaneously instilling a sense of community between the totalitarian dictatorship and the German population, an attempt to improve the status of workers and their conditions to compensate for wage freezes, longer working hours (up to 60 hour work weeks) and restrictions on private consumption

98

OG-37 L = 210 mm / 8 1/4"

OG-37   DAF SdA - I.G. Farben N.W.7

Tablespoon: The obverse is marked with Farben's emblem of "I" over "G" with "Berlin N.W.7." below. Reverse carries the maker mark of Tc & 'MDA SchdA', & ROSTFREI.

I.G. Farben was a conglomerate that before WW I had a near monopoly on world dyestuffs. Per chapter two of 'The Empire of I.G. Farben': "The Berlin N.W. 7 office (Unter den Linden 82) of I.G. Farben was the key Nazi overseas intelligence, espionage and propaganda center prior to WWII. One of the more prominent of these Farben intelligence workers (verbindungsmanner / liaison men) in N.W. 7 was Prince Bernhard of the Netherlands, who joined Farben in the early 1930s after completion of an 18-month period of service in the S.S."   N. W. 7 operated under Farben director Max Ilgner, nephew of I.G. Farben president Hermann Schmitz. Max Ilgner and Hermann Schmitz were on the board of American I.G., with other directors Henry Ford of Ford Motor Company, Paul Warburg of Bank of Manhattan, and Charles E. Mitchell of the Federal Reserve Bank of New York. In 1939, of 43 major I. G. products 28 were of "primary concern" to the German armed forces. Prior to the invasions of Czechoslovakia and Poland, IG identified specific chemical plants to be delivered to Farben. At the Nuremberg trials of IG in 1947/48, "Berlin N.W.7" was identified as, "the Nazi prewar intelligence office" which resulted in sentences of Schmitz 4 years, Ilgner 3 years. Note: By 1944, the Farben Auschwitz factory complex had employed some 83,000 forced laborers of which 40,000 perished. The Buna facility produced 100% of Germany's synthetic rubber and 45% of its aviation gasoline from coal.

ps. Hitler, Goering and The Reich Ministry of Economics were in Berlin postal code W.8. while Himmler & Heydrich were at Berlin S.W. 11.

OG-38
L = 210 mm / 8 1/4"

OG-38 DAF SdA - Bra AG

Tablespoon: Obverse plain with a raised central spine and
carries the logo Bra AG. Reverse has the DAF wheel with a
mobile swastika and below the initials MDA (Modell Des
Amtes / Model of the Office) and below that SchdA
(Schonheit der Arbeit / Beauty of Labor. Maker marked Tc
and RUSTFREI.

The Bra AG logo is unknown but the spoon recently came
from Poland and may have been a company in the East of
pre war Germany.

The SdA (Speer) decided what constituted good industrial
design, ie simplicity of line etc. The majority of the cutlery
carried organizational logos on either the obverse or reverse
such as BMW for the cutlery at their Munick factory or like
the early Berlin N.W 7 - I. G. Farben, even Luftwaffe eagles.
Others carried no logo.

Nazi's rejected:
    Marxist "Class Conflict" as a violation of their vision of a
        unified racial community and
    "Fordism" (consumerism) which placed little value on
        German "Quality" work, worshiped commodities
        and instant gratification of individual wants.

SdA embraced the totality of the workers "creative lives" with
emphasis on the workplace as the key to regulating leisure
time and disciplining consumption. SdA was less able to
build popular support for the regime due to the inherent
coercion of SdA's plant communities by emphasis on "pride
of work" vs material rewards.

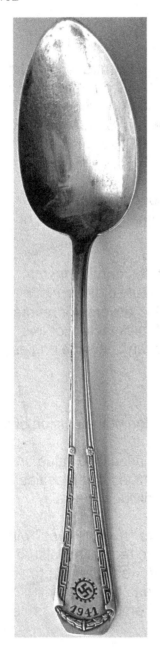

OG-39
L = 183 mm / 7 1/4"

OG-39 DAF (Deutsche Arbeitsfront)

Spoon: Obverse carries DAF emblem over '1941'. Reverse with Reichsmark, 800 and maker marked of Gebruder Koberlin, Dobeln founded 1828

The Deutsche Arbeitsfront (abbr. DAF, often translated to German Labor Front) was founded on 10 May 1933 under the patronage of Hitler and directed by Robert Ley, Reichsorganisationsleiter der NSDAP as the Nazi's substitute organization for trade unions that were made illegal after their rise to power in 1933. It soon grew to be a giant bureaucratic machine with 25 million members and 40,000 staff with a considerable influence within the Nazi regime. Conceived as an alternative to trade unions, it was supposed to be representative of employers and employees alike. However, in reality it was a means by which workers were controlled, ensuring wage demands were not made and that the position of the employer was the 'leader' with the worker cast as 'follower'. Wages were set by the 12 DAF trustees, who followed the will of the employers. It became part of the NSDAP organization in October 1934, having its base in Berlin

Within the DAF, several sub-organizations were set up:

> Kraft durch Freude (KdF; Strength through Joy)
> Schönheit der Arbeit (SdA; Beauty of Work)
> Reichsarbeitsdienst (RAD; Reich Labour Service)

In 1937 Robert Ley, stated DAF's aim as "to create a true social and productive community" and on Hitler in 1938 "I believe on this earth in Adolf Hitler alone. I believe in one Lord God who made me and guides me, and I believe that this Lord God has sent Adolf Hitler to us."

OG-40 DAF (Deutsche Arbeitsfront)
(7 Piece Set)

Obverse carries the DAF logo. Reverse maker marked
GEBR.HEPP and '90'

This group (dinner knife, dinner spoon, dinner fork, salad
fork, teaspoon, serving spatula and lobster fork) is reportedly
from the former headquarters building of DAF located at
Berlin's Potsdamer Strasse 182 and the original building is
still in use today.

There were 2 main components of the DAF:
 * Nationalsozialistische Betriebszellenorganisation
     (NSBO; National Socialist Factory Organization)
 * Nationalsozialistische Handels und
     Gewerbeorganization (NSHABO; National Socialist
     Trade and Industry Organization)

Several other sub-organisations were set up:
 * Kraft durch Freude (KdF; Strength through Joy) –
Organization giving the workers cheap/free holidays in
addition to subsidized sporting and leisure facilities.
    *Schönheit der Arbeit (SdA; Beauty of Work) – Aimed to
make workplaces more enticing to workers (e.g. renovations
of outdated factories, new canteens for workers, smoking-
free rooms, cleaner working spaces etc.).
    *Reichsarbeitsdienst (RAD; Reich Labor Service) A
Solution to the unemployment crisis the Nazis inherited.
Provided cheap labor for big state projects, such as the
Autobahns. Made compulsory for unemployed men 16-25 in
1935. Provided work security to many unemployed.

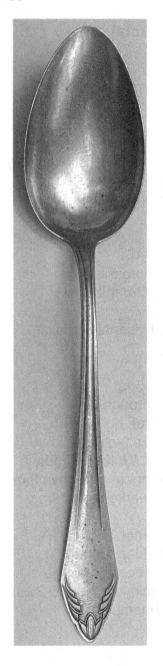

OG-41
L = 207 mm / 8 2/16"

OG-41 Dh - Dienststelle Heismeyer?

Tablespoon, Obverse with flower detail on tip. Reverse with right looking eagle over 'Dh' and maker marked Br Henneberg BM and '40' in a circle.

Reference PS-14, the 'Dh' logo is associated with Bernard Rust and education generally. Another association could be with Hauptamt Dienststelle SS-Obergruppenführer Heißmeyer. The National Political Institutes of Education (Nationalpolitische Erziehungsanstalten); officially abbreviated NPEA, were secondary boarding schools in Nazi Germany founded as "community education sites" after the National Socialist seizure of power in 1933. The goal of the schools was to raise a new generation for the political, military, and administrative leadership of the Nazi state. Only boys and girls considered to be "racially flawless" were admitted to the boarding schools. No children with poor hearing or vision were accepted. "Above-average intelligence" was also required, so those seeking admission had to complete 8-day entrance exams. The first three NPEA's were founded in 1933 by the Minister of Education Bernhard Rust in Plön, Potsdam, and Köslin. The schools reported directly to the Reich Ministry for Education, rather than to any states like regular schools. From 1936, the NPEA's were subordinated to the Inspector of the National Political Institutes of Education, SS Obergruppenführer August Heissmeyer. With the outbreak of WWII, Heissmeyer set up the "Dienststelle SS-Obergruppenführer Heissmeyer" – his own bureau – and was thereby responsible for NPEA students' military training. The schools were now under the direct influence of the SS. Boys eventually entered the SS in much higher rates (13%) than in the general German population of 1.8%. In 1941, there were a total of 30 NPEA's with 6,000 students enrolled in all of Nazi Germany.

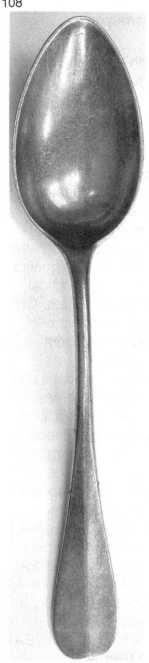

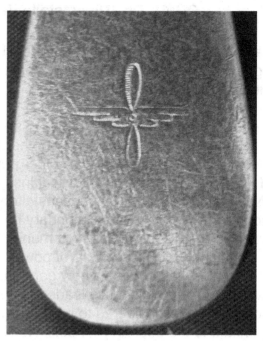

OG-42
L = 184 mm / 7 3/16"

OG-42 DLV - Deutscher Luftfahrt Verband
(German Aviation League)

Dessert spoon (10 ml): Obverse is unmarked with a raised spine. Reverse carries the early emblem (1922-33) of the DLV and has a style mark of "30" in a square, the silver plating indicator of '90' in a circle, "Berndorf", a standing bear in a circle and the letter 'L' for their Swiss plant in Luzern.

The Deutscher Luftfahrt Verband (DLV) was founded in 1922. It was a civilian aviation club promoting both sport and commercial aviation. in 1933, under the Nazi's, it became the Deutscher Luftsport Verband or German Air-Sport League and added a mobile swastika on the propeller hub . The DLV was very closely associated with the Hitler Youth. Events involved model building with flying competitions of the completed projects, aeronautical educational classes followed by building and flying actual glider aircraft. The DLV was divided into three sections - powered flight, gliders and ballooning. The DLV owned sixteen gliding aviation schools and three larger State Soaring Schools. Under the Nazi's this was a covert organization for the training of both pilots and support personnel for the, then secret, Luftwaffe. In April 1933 Hitler's pilot Captain Hans Bauer, usually described as 'bibulous', sported the DLV uniform which had been personally approved by Hermann Goering and was later adopted with slight modification by the Luftwaffe. By the time Hitler officially called for volunteers for the Luftwaffe in March 1935, there were actually some 1,888 aircraft of all types and some 20,000 officers and men who quickly changed from the DLV uniform to the Luftwaffe uniform, On 17 April 1937, the DLV was disbanded and was superseded by the NSFK Nationalsozialistisches Fliegerkorps (National Socialist Flying Corps).

OG-43   L = 141 mm / 5 9/16"

OG-43 DR - Deutsche Reichsbahn
(German National Railways)

Teaspoon: On the obverse is the modified DR emblem where the original flanged wheel has been replaced by a mobile swastika which became mandatory in 1937, Reverse carries RM, 800 and maker's mark GR (Gebruder Reiner, Krumbach Bayern 1910 - present).

During World War II, the Reichsbahn was an essential component of German military logistics, providing transportation services for the Reich throughout the occupied lands of Europe and employed 1,600,000.

The DR was not included in Armament planning until 1941. In 1942 it was assigned 'Highest Priority" along with 69,500 tons of steel monthly to produce 500 locomotives monthly. In 1943 its priority was superseded by the "Adolf Hitler Tank Program", a commitment Hitler made to the Heer.

In the East:

By 1 Sep 1939 - The DR had moved 86 non motorized divisions to the Polish border. During the Polish campaign, both sides participated in the destruction of the Polish rail system. The program to double the existing capacity for the invasion of Russia started In Oct 1940. By June 1941, east traffic was raised from 84 to 220 trains a day. 141 German divisions were moved to the Soviet border without detection.

From the Invasion of Russia on 22 June 1941 to 1 Jan 1943, the DR converted 22,000 miles of Soviet wide gauge rail to German standard gauge. East bound trains from Germany, daily: Dec41 = 122, 1Jan42 = 140 and 1Mar42 = 180 or a train to the East front every 8 minutes!

OG-44 DR - Deutsche Reichsbahn
(Hitler's Private Dining Car)

Tablespoon and matching teaspoon from Hitler's private dining car. The spoons obverse carries the "DR" logo, on the reverse the spoon is maker marked: RM, 800, eagle of Bruckmann & Sohne., followed by a large '205' indicating it is from Sonderzug / Fuhrerzug car #10205 / #205.

This train pattern was used on the German National Railroad. Prior to 1939, Hitler's private train was labeled Fuhrerzug - Leader's Train. In 1939, Hitler's 1st Wartime Headquarters was placed on the 17 car Fuhrersonderzug or Leader's Special Train. All the coaches were specially constructed of welded steel and therefore weighing in at over 60 tons each. Hitler's private Pullman car was #10206 and was fitted out to Hitler's own specifications. Car #10205 (the executive, private dining car with rose wood paneling and indirect lighting) was abbreviated as 205 on the car's china, flatware, silver serving pieces, and linens. The cutlery carries the Bruckmann maker's mark while, the porcelain was maker marked: Nymphenburg. A 2nd dining car for staff and enlisted men was # 10213, abbreviated as 213 on the associated flatware. The train was code named "Fuhrersonderzug F' until 1940, then "Amerika" from a French town near Hitler's WWI location and finally "Brandenburg". His 206 Pullman car was blown up by German Army engineers in April 1945 on Hitler's orders.

Note: There were two full time silver polishers assigned to the Fuhrersonderzug!

OG-44 & 45
Tablespoon = 211 mm / 8 5/16", Tea 140 mm / 5 1/2"

OG-45 DR - Deutsche Reichsbahn
Details of Hitler's private dining car's silverware.

In 1924, the Deutsche Reichbahn was created as a state enterprise under the Reich Ministry of Transportation. On 10 Feb 1937, the Nazi government took total control of the rail network. To emphasize this, swastikas were added to the Hoheitsadler (sovereignty eagle) - the traditional symbol of Germany on all railcars, and the initials "DR" were held to stand for "Deutsches Reich" but were construed to be for "Deutsches Reichbahn.   Maker marks identical to OG-42

> Trivia: Hitler's Fuhrersonderzug sleeping carriage 10222 survived the war and was used by the President's of the Federal Republic of Germany into the 1980's.

Special DR Note: The DR's participation was crucial to the implementation of the "Final Solution of the Jewish Question". The Reichsbahn was paid to transport victims of the Holocaust from towns and cities throughout Europe to the Nazi concentration camp system and were paid by the track kilometer, so many pfennigs per Km. The rate was the same throughout the war. With children under ten going at half-fare and children under four going free. Payment had to be made for only one way. The guards of course had to have return fare paid for them because they were going back to their place of origin. Slovakia paid the SS 500 RM / $ 200 for the transportation of each of the 60,000 deported Slovakian jews that were sent to the concentration camps.

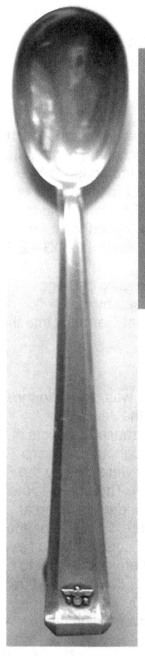

OG-46
L = 122 mm / 4 13/16"

OG-46 DR - Deutsche Reichsbahn
(Enlisted Men's Dining Car #213)

Demitasse sugar spoon: Obverse carries the "DR" eagle with the swastika straddled by the 'D' and 'R'. The reverse carries the Fuhrersonderzug's number 213 identifying it as from the enlisted personnel's dining car with RM, 800 and a Bruckmann & Sohne eagle maker's mark.

Some additional details regards the Fuhrersonderzug: The sequence of cars was subject to minor modifications but it typically was composed as: Cars 1 & 2 were two steam locomotives in tandem. Car 3 was a flakwagon (armored railroad car), each end open with a 4 barreled M-1938 20 mm cannon manned by 26 Luftwaffe personnel. Car 4 was a combination baggage and auxiliary power car. Car 5 was the Fuhrer's Pullman No 10206. Car 6 the Befehlswagen (command car) which included a conference room with map tables and a separate communications compartment. Car 7 the Begleitkommandowagen (escort) car for Hitler's 22 man FuhrerBegleit-Kommando and the RSD personnel. Car 8 the Executive dining car No 10205. Cars 9 & 10 sleeping cars for guests and entourage. Car 11 Badewagon (bathing car). Car 12 enlisted mens dining car No. 10213. Cars 13 & 14 sleeping cars for enlisted men. Car 15 Presswagen (Press chief Otto Dietrich's car). Car 16 another baggage and power generator car. Last Car 17 a second flakwagon.

First used for the Polish campaign with the thought that it could be rapidly deployed West in case France were to attack. On board were Hitler's military adjutants, liaison officers, party officials, Generals Keital (IQ 129) and Jodl. (IQ 127). (The Generals would have their own trains shortly.) Hitler's last train ride was from FHQ Adlerhorst to Berlin on 15 January 1945.

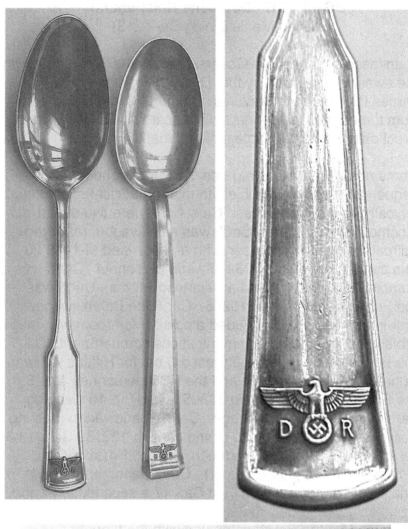

OG-47   L = 216 mm / 8 1/2"

OG-47 DR - Deutsche Reichsbahn
Table spoon from Goering's private dining car.

As with Hitler but on a grander scale, Herman Goering's
two personal trains were in Obersalzburg in April 1945. His
primary private dining car was number 10243 '243'. Other
cars were '233', '234' and '244'. This tablespoon carries the
Goring dining car number '243' and is maker marked:
Capital 'B' (Bruckmann) with a locomotive symbol followed
by a '90'. There have recently surfaced a number of the
raised edge 243 spoons which are now the most prevalently
available. The demonstrably different shape of this Goering
spoon is evident when set side by side with the A. H. DR
spoon and is generally described as with 'raised edge'.

> Trivia: Goering's Sonderzuge were first named *Asien I*
> and *Asien II* and later renamed *Pommern I* and
> *Pommern II*.

> Note: I have recently seen DR cutlery marked 244 and
> identical in form to the Hitler 205 above.

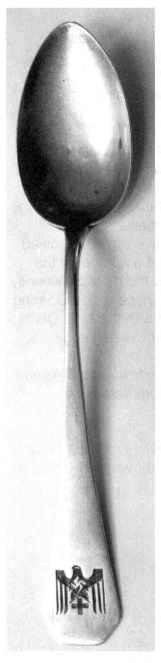

OG-48
L = 136 mm / 5 6/16"

OG-48 DRK -.Deutsches Rotes Kreuz
(German Red Cross)

Teaspoon. The spoon carries the DRK logo on the obverse and maker marked on the reverse: "CB 800" and RM.

Originally a voluntary civil assistance organization started in 1864. The NSDAP recognized the DRK in December 1937 and took control in 1938. During the Third Reich, the DRK emblem had a black eagle with elongated down swept wings and a white, mobile swastika superimposed on its breast, clutching a red Balkan cross (known in English as a Greek cross - a cross with straight lines) in its talons while the standard international red cross flag was also still utilized to denote first aid and medical locations.

DRK Trivia - typical of Nazi protocol, daggers were a standard item of dress. Due to its noncombatant status, the DRK had to conform to the international Geneva convention which directed that members not carry any weapons, including edged weapons. As a result, the DRK 'Subordinates Hewer', introduced in 1938, was designed with a squared blunt tip and blunt scabbard to preclude its classification as a weapon and allowed its wear in the field. The DRK Leaders dagger, with a pointed tip and pointed scabbard, was classified as a weapon and could only be worn as a dress dagger, when not in the field.

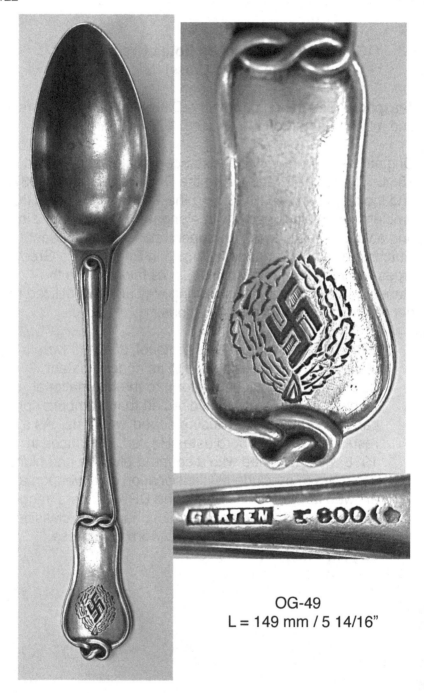

OG-49
L = 149 mm / 5 14/16"

OG-49 National-Socialistische Deutsche Studenten Bund - NSDStB
(National Socialist Student Federation)

Teaspoon. This teaspoon carries the Studentenbund Ehrenzeichen (Student Federation Decoration) on the obverse The reverse is maker marked 'GARTEN' 800, RM. This decoration has no eagle . The NSDStB emblem has the eagle clasping their elongated swastika as per the Sport Shirt Patch photo below. There is also a stylized initial H on the reverse as per below.

All German students at the universities were required to belong to the Studentenschaft (Student Corps). The Student Corps was responsible for making the students conscious of their duties to the Nazis State and was obliged to promote enrollment in the SA and labor service. Physical training of students was the responsibility of the SA. Political education was the responsibility of the National-Socialistische Deutsche Studentenbund (NSDStB), (National Socialist German Student Bund) and was the Nazi "elite" of the student body and responsible for the leadership of the university students, and all leaders of the Student Corps were appointed from its membership. The Nazi Student Bund was solely responsible for the entire ideological and political education of the students.

OG-50
L = 142 mm / 5 5/8"

OG-50   National Socialist Student Federation (National-Socialistische Deutsche Studenten Bund) - NSDStB

Teaspoon. This teaspoon's obverse carries a hand engraved simplest / minimalist Studentenbund Ehrenzeichen (Student Federation Decoration). Reverse Maker marked: Vereinigte Silberwarenfabriken, Dusseldorf, founded 1899, '800', RM.

The NSDStB was originally formed as a semiautonomous National Socialist organization in 1926, infiltrating the majority of institutions by 1930 and was under full control of the Nazi party by 1934.

OG-51
L = 178 mm / 7"

OG-51 NSKK - Nationasozialistisches Kraftfahrkorps
(National Socialist Motor Corps)

Table fork: Obverse carries the NSKK logo. Reverse with maker mark of a stylized 'A' over 'H', followed by 'HANS 90-30'.

The National Socialist Motor Corps, (NSKK), began on 1 Apr 1930 when the Nationalsozialistisches Automobil Korps (NSAK) was founded on the order of Martin Bormann as a paramilitary organization of the Nazi Party. It was to organize all NSDAP members who owned a car or motorcycle in a single nation–wide unit. SA-Gruppenführer Adolf Hühnlein was made commander of the NSAK and suggested renaming it NSKK and this was accepted by SA-leader Ernst Röhm who was in the process of reorganizing the SA. When Adolf Hitler became chancellor in 1933 the NSKK expanded rapidly to 30,000 members. After Röhm and the SA-leadership were murdered during the Night of Long Knives (30 June 1934) the Motor-SA became a part of the NSKK and it was made an independent organization. The NSKK took over all German motor clubs Sep 1933 and expanded to 350,000 members. After Austria was made a part of Germany (Mar 1938) the NSKK expanded to over 500,000 members. With the outbreak of World War II in 1939, the National Socialist Motor Corps became a target of the Wehrmacht for recruitment, since NSKK members possessed knowledge of motorized transport, whereas the bulk of the Wehrmacht relied on horses. Most NSKK members thereafter joined the regular military, serving in the transport corps of the various service branches. In 1945, the NSKK was disbanded and the group was declared a "condemned organization" at the Nuremberg Trials (although not a criminal one). This was due in part to the NSKK's origins in the SA and its doctrine of racial superiority required from its members.

128

OG-52
L = 217 mm / 8 9/16"

OG-52   NS-Kriegsopferversorgung
NSKOV
National Socialist War Victim's Welfare Service)

Soupspoon: The obverse carries the NSKOV shield decoration composed of a black mobile swastika within a circle and the circle set against a black iron cross all within a shield. The reverse carries the maker mark of Koch & Bergfeld, Bremen, founded 1829, 800, RM.

The NSKOV (National Socialist War Victim's Welfare Service or War Disabled Support Organization) was established in 1930 and institutionalized in 1935 as a social welfare organization to assist NSDAP party members who had become disabled as a result of First World War injuries.

Although an NSDAP affiliated charity, it maintained a degree of independence in assets and organizational issues. Together with the National Peoples Welfare (NSV) it was a charitable organization and supported health programs from its establishment till 1945.

By Law No. 5 (The Denazification Decree) of the American Military Government dated 31 May 1945, the NAZI Party with all its institutions and organizations were disbanded.

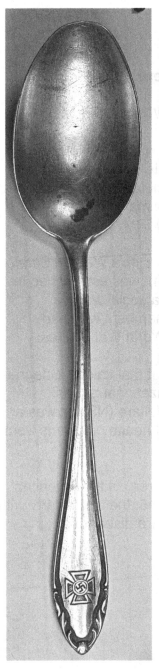

OG-53
L = 139 mm / 5 1/2"

OG-53   NS-Kriegsopferversorgung
NSKOV
(National Socialist War Victim's Welfare Service)

Teaspoon: The obverse carries the basic NSKOV decoration composed of a black mobile swastika within a circle and the circle set against a black iron cross. Reverse carries an unidentified maker's mark of capital 'E" in a lozenge, 800, RM.

The Nationalsozialistische Kriegsopferversorgung (NSKOV), meaning "National Socialist War Victim's Care" was a social welfare organization for seriously wounded veterans as well as frontline fighters of World War I. The NSKOV was established in 1934 and was affiliated to the NSDAP.

After Nazi Germany's defeat in World War II, the American Military Government issued a special law outlawing the Nazi party and all of its branches. Known as "Law number five", this Denazification decree disbanded the NSKOV, like all organizations linked to the Nazi Party. The organizations taking care of the welfare for World War I veterans had to be established anew during the postwar reconstruction of both West Germany and the DDR.

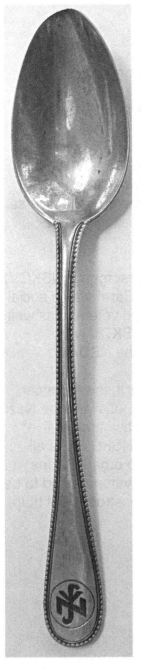

OG-54
L = 144 mm / 5 11/16"

133

OG-54 Nationalsozialistische Volkswohlfahrt (NSV)
(National Socialist People's Welfare)

Teaspoon: Obverse carries the NSV Logo. Reverse with
C.A. Krall makers mark, 800 RM.

The NSV was established on 3 May 1933, shortly after the
NSDAP took power and was the umbrella organization for a
range of social and welfare programs, at first helping poor
families with food and fuel, gradually shifting to performing
services such as organizing and managing day care centers,
caring for children, assistance to youth and pregnant
women, and various family health and nutrition programs.
The NSV was financed through voluntary contributions such
as the Nazi Winter Support Program (Winterhilfswerk). With
the advent of the War, the program was massively
expanded, so that the régime deemed it worthy to be called
the "greatest social institution in the world." One method of
expansion was to absorb, or in NSDAP parlance coordinate,
already existing but non-Nazi charity organizations such as
church run day care centers. The NSV became the principal
national effort devoted to children and youth welfare efforts
which increased membership from 1 million in 1938 to 11
million making it the second largest Nazi group organization
by 1939, second only to the German Labor Front.

Note: 1. A major slogan at NSV day care centers was
       "Hände falten, Köpfchen senken - immer an Adolf
       Hitler denken "-- Hands folded, head lowered -
       always of Adolf Hitler thinking".

       2. Winter Support Program slogan: "None shall
       starve nor freeze".

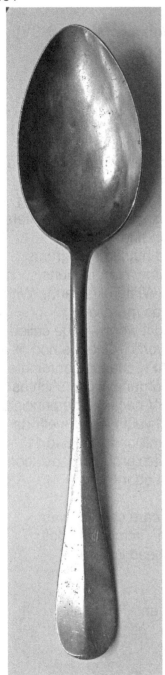

OG-55
L = 217 mm / 8 9/16"

OG-55 RAD - Reichs Arbeitsdienst
(National Labor-Service).

Tablespoon. This Mess Hall tablespoon (Essloffel). Marked
on the reverse side with "REICHSARBEITSDIENST" "1936".
Manufactured by Duralit and of stainless steel (Rostfrie).

RAD basis dates back to 1929's formation of AAD "Anhalt
Arbeitsdienst" (Anhalt Labor-Service) and the FAD-B,
"Freiwillingen Arbeitsdienst-Bayern" (Volunteer Labor-
Service [of] Bavaria). In 1933, the NSDAP consolidated
labor organizations into the NSAD, "Nationalsozialist
Arbietsdienst" (National-Socialist Labor-Service); a national
labor service. In June 1935, NSAD was re-designated RAD,
in July RAD service became compulsory for both young men
(prior to military service) and women, with all German
citizens between 19 and 25 required to enlist for a 6 month
term and military conscripts to serve 9 months. Typical work
projects were road construction and farm labor.

The RAD motto: ArbeitAdelt - Work Ennobles.

OG-56
L = 215 mm / 8 1/2"

OG-56 RAD - Reichs Arbeitsdienst
(National Labor-Service).

Fork, Mess Hall (Kantine Gabel): Obverse is clear with a raised central spine. Reverse carries the RAD symbol of a shovel and 'Art Krupp"NICAD' 'Berndorf' '1941'. Note: 'Art" was supposedly dropped in 1938 do to his death.

Reichsarbeitsdienst, 'RAD' (National Labor Service) was under the Deutsche Arbeitsfront, 'DAF' (German Labor Service). In 1931, to combat German unemployment, a voluntary work service was formed. When Hitler was made Chancellor 1933 he soon appointed Konstantin Hierl as Secretary of State for the Labor Service, the control of which at this time were transferred from the states to the central government. The RAD was formally founded on 26 June 1935 making service in the RAD compulsory. RAD's mission was to provide labor for public projects for both civil and military projects mainly for reclaiming land for farming, helping with the harvests and construction of roads, but also for various emergency relief projects. In 1939, the RAD lost over half of its men to the armed forces. During the war, RAD was classified as a reserve troop, an auxiliary to the Wehrmacht, not actually in the armed forces but close enough to be protected by the Geneva convention. Major activities were focused on the supply to the front lines of food and ammunitions, repairing roads, construction and repair of Luftwaffe airfields. Eventually, RAD personnel were drawn into active military service, especially on the East front where by the wars end, there were eight major RAD front line units in service.

Motto: Working men are healthy, happy, self-conscious work soldiers.

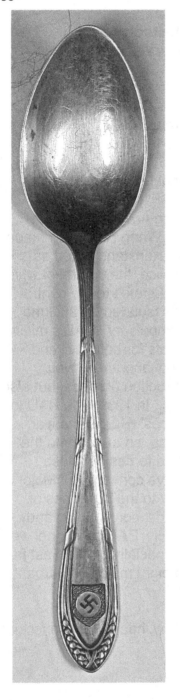

OG-57
L = 138 mm / 5 7/16"

OG-57 RAD Reichsarbeitsdienst (German Labor Service)

Teaspoon, Thanks to _Treasures of the Third Reich_'s Dan Kelley for the following analysis of the obverse: "Note on your spoon handle the shape of a shovel and the wheat stalks wrapping around the edge of the spoon, this has all of the imagery of the RAD or Reichs Arbeitsdienst; the German Workers Service." The reverse marked 800, Reichsmark and maker mark of Gebruder Koberlin, Dobeln, founded 1828.

With the war, the RAD was classed as Wehrmachtgefolge (lit. Armed Forces Auxiliaries). Auxiliary forces with this status, while not a part of the Armed Forces themselves, provided such vital support that they were given protection by the Geneva Convention. Some, including the RAD, were militarized.

During the early war's Norwegian and Western campaigns, hundreds of RAD units were engaged in supplying frontline troops with food and ammunition, repairing damaged roads and constructing and repairing airstrips. Throughout the course of the war, the RAD was involved in many projects. The RAD units constructed coastal fortifications (many RAD men worked on the Atlantic Wall), laid minefields, staffed fortifications, and even helped guard vital locations and prisoners.

The role of the RAD was not limited to combat support functions. Hundreds of RAD units received training as anti-aircraft units and were deployed as RAD Flak Batteries. Several RAD units also performed combat on the eastern front as infantry. As the German defenses were devastated, more and more RAD men were committed to combat. During the final months of the war RAD men formed 6 major frontline units, which were involved with serious fighting.<w>

OG-58
L = 238 mm / 9 5/16"

OG-58 RAD Reichsarbeitsdienst (German Labor Service)

Knife: Obverse clear. Reverse marked 'RAD'. maker marked H.M.Z. 37 and blade marked HMZ Rustfrei.

The Nazi's viewed manual labor as a way to break down social and class barriers and to mold the character of young people, "the dignity of manual labor".

A 1935 law required all Aryan Germans (ages 17-25) to serve in the RAD for 6 months. Thus, prior to the war it was a program to create jobs for unemployed youth.

The RAD was divided into two major sections:
> Reichsarbeitsdienst Männer (RAD/M) for men
> Reichsarbeitdienst der weiblichen Jugend (RAD/wJ) for women.

The RAD was composed of 40 districts each called an Arbeitsgau (lit. Work District). Each of these districts was headed by an officer with headquarters staff and a Wachkompanie (Guard Company). Under each district were between six and eight Arbeitsgruppen (Workers Groups), battalion-sized formations of 1200-1800 men. These groups were divided into six company-sized RAD-Abteilung units. Each rank and file RAD man was supplied with a spade and a bicycle. The RAD symbol, an arm badge in the shape of an upward pointing shovel blade, was displayed on the upper left shoulder of all uniforms and great-coats worn by all personnel. The pre war RAD undertook the construction of the Autobahn as well as other roads, land reclamation as well as the construction of military installations. <w>

OG-59
L = 210 mm / 8 5/16"

OG-59 'R.K' - Reichs-Kanzlei
(The New Reich Chancellery)

Tablespoon. The obverse of this table service (besteck) has the eagle facing to his right, legs apart on a static swastika in the double wreath with an 'R' on the left and on the right a 'K'. There is no Greek key design. The reverse carries the RM, 800 and Bruckmann eagle. This is official, silver Besteck, from the **'New' Reich Chancellery** / (Neureichskanzlei, Interestingly, although Wellner's "AH" had only one eagle, the Bruckmann's "RK" had both "Straight Wing" and "Swept Wing" (spread) eagles.

This was Hitler's Berlin chancellery and one of his official residences where all the most important state affairs were conducted. When present, Hitler used his formal 'AH' pattern, (see PS-1) otherwise, only the likes of Mussolini, Ciano, Chamberlain, Goring, Goebbels and Himmler used this flatware when the Fuhrer himself was not seated. Probably 100 times more rare than the 'AH' formal pattern. Considered a museum piece as the Chancellery was destroyed by fire in 1945 and afterwards occupied by the Russians so that very little survived. Shown here with a companion fork.

RK trivia: The cost of construction was estimated to be $ 100 million equivalent to $ 1 billion today. Hitler was very impressed when Speer managed both the design and had it constructed in a few days shy of one year by coordinating multiple construction teams working in parallel. The classic of "Nazi Architecture".

OG-60
L = 138 mm / 5 7/16"

OG-60 RKB - Reichskolonialbund
(German Colonial League)

Teaspoon. Obverse carries the emblem of the RKB - Reichskolonialbund. On the reverse, 800, RM, and the maker mark of Gebruder Koberlin, Dobeln, Founded 1828.

The RKB was established on 13 June 1936 to "keep the population informed about the loss of the German Imperial colonies, to maintain contact with former colonial territories and to create conditions in opinion favorable to a new German African Empire." The aim was to claim back the overseas colonies that Germany had lost as a result of the Treaty of Versailles.

Since Germany had no colonies, the Reichskolonialbund was mainly engaged in mostly virulent political agitation, primarily in Germany. This in an effort to keep open the "Koloniale Frage" (Colonial Question).

The League had its own youth organization, the Kolonialjugend which was incorporated as a wing of the Hitler Youth.

With WWII, the League began to decline as the Nazi State was focused on other higher priorities. In 1943, Reichsleiter Martin Bormann pressed for the dissolution of the League on the grounds of "kriegsunwichtiger Tatigkeit" (activity irrelevant to the war). The Reichskolonialbund was swiftly disbanded by virtue of a decree of the Fuhrer in 1943.

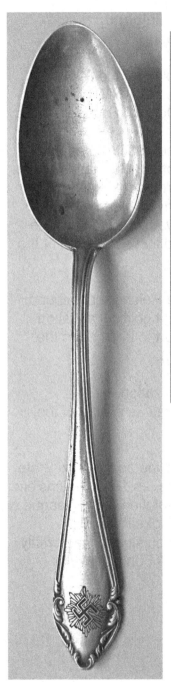

OG-61
L = 142 mm / 5 10/16

147

OG-61 Reichs Luftschutzbund
(National Air Raid Protection League)

Teaspoon. The obverse carries the decoration of a mobile swastika in an ornate 48 point white star burst background as illustrated in Brian Davis's *'Badges & Insignia of the Third Reich'*, plate 34, item #16 and is identified as the second pattern used by the RLB from 1938. Maker marked: Vereinigte Silberwarenfabriken, Dusseldorf, founded 1899, '800', RM.

Reichs Luftschutzbund (National Air Protection League) Originally formed in late 1932, the Deutscher Luftschutzverband (German Air Protection League) was a voluntary organization designed to provide civil air raid protection in large civilian centers. In 1933 it was placed under the supervision of Hermann Goering's Reichsluftfahrt Ministerium (National Air Ministry). On 29 April 1933 the DLB was re-designated the Reichs Luftschutz Bund (National Air Raid Protection League) or RLB, now responsible for all aspects of civil air raid defense. Voluntary up to June 1935 - when obligatory service was established.

Note: The 1st pattern RLB emblem (circa 1933-38) was a 48 point white star burst pattern with stylized "RLB" initials to the center positioned above a small mobile swastika. In October 1938 the RLB emblem was redesigned and replaced the RLB letters with a large swastika and was used till the end of the war

148

WELLNER PATENT 90 131

OG-62
L = 238 mm / 9 6/16"

OG-62 RMJ - Reichministerium der Justiz
(German Ministry of Justice)

Serving Spoon. Obverse carries the "Ministry of Justice" logo while the reverse is maker marked Wellner Patent 90 3.

The four Nazis who bore much of the responsibility for allowing the legal system of Germany to be taken over by Nazi ideology were Franz Schlegelburger (RMJ 1941-42), Roland Freisler. Otto Thierack (RMJ 1943-45) and Curt Rothenberger.

At the 1946 Nuremberg 'Judges' Trial, Schlegelberger was one of the main accused, He helped create the "Enabling Act" of 21Mar1933 to strengthen the executive. Helped pass the 13July1934 retroactive law justifying the "Night of the Long Knives" murders of 30 June which effectively established Hitler above the law. In August 1934, all judges and public prosecutors were bound to Hitler by an oath of loyalty. During his time in office he authored bills such as the (Polenstrafrechtsverordnung) so called Poland Penal Law Provision under which Poles were executed for tearing down German posters. He sharply increased German death sentences and by 1943 there were 46 Capital Offense Crimes with the death penalty including: listening to foreign broadcasts, engaging in rumors, having or aiding an abortion and scavenging rubble. He was sentenced to life in prison for conspiracy to perpetrate war crimes and crimes against humanity.

Hitler's earliest direction to the judiciary was to protect the interests of the Volk (nation) above those of the individual.

Note: Serving spoons are always the rarest of any assemblage since there is usually only one or two to a set.

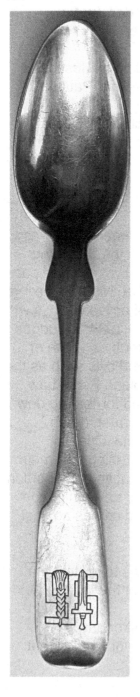

OG-63
L = 147 mm / 5 13/16"

OG-63 RNS - Reichs Nahrstand
(German Food Corporation)

Teaspoon. Obverse carries the Reichs Nahrstand logo while the reverse "Proll' 800 & unknown maker mark

The German Food Corporation was created on 13Sep1933 when all previous agricultural associations and organizations were disbanded. Walter Darre, (SS-Obergruppenfuhrer) the leading ideologist of Blut und Boden (Blood / Descent and Soil / Homeland) was the Reichminister of Food from 1933 to 1942. He had come to Hitler's attention via his 1929 book: *The Peasantry as a Life Source of the Nordic Race.* Focused on the peasantry as the life source of the Nordic race, the goal was to preserve a healthy peasant stock via the compulsory organization of agriculture which took total control of the markets and prices as well as stabilized ownership of land. The farmers were organized into this grandiose sounding, nationally directed agrarian estate - the Nahrstand.

It eventually was perceived by the farmers as a bureaucratic encroachment on their autonomy and due to restrictions on land sales, forced the farmers to remain farmers. As unemployment decreased: Oct 1933 - 6.0 Million, Oct 1934 - 4.1 Million and Feb 1935 - 2.8 Million, available farm labor became a problem leading to higher labor costs and reduced production which made autarky or independence of imports from other nations unattainable. In spite of all efforts, prior to the outbreak of WWII, agricultural self sufficiency never exceeded 80%.

Note: In 1937, although farmers were 22 % of the German population they made up only 9 % of the SS which was noted by the responsible authorities.

Wehrmacht Introduction
(Armed Services)

Per Wikipedia: Wehrmacht ("Defense Forces" or more literally "Defense Power") was the name of the unified armed forces of Germany from 1935 to 1945. It consisted of the Heer (Army), the Kriegsmarine (Navy) and the Luftwaffe (Air Force).

The Waffen-SS, an initially-small paramilitary section of Heinrich Himmler's Allgemeine SS that grew to nearly a million strong during World War II, was not part of the Wehrmacht, but under operational command of the OKW (Oberkommando der Wehrmacht / German Armed Forces Supreme Command ie Hitler as of 4Feb1938) and OKH (Heer).

Albert Kesselring, (Smiling Albert) Luftwaffe Field Marshal summed up the philosophical differences between the 3rd Reich's Defense services as: "the 'republican' Army, the 'imperialist' Navy and the 'national socialist' Luftwaffe." These adjectives reveal the patent disunity of the Service's attitudes.

These 'disparate attitudes' can be seen in their tableware via the presentation of the Nazi swastika to the traditional national eagle via the Army's middle of the road, the Navy's minimal and the Luftwaffe's excessive presentation of the swastika.

German Military Philosophy

German military success was to be based on superior leadership, organization, supply and morale. This was believed to overcome material / manpower limitations. In War and Peace, Leo Tolstoy observed that the effectiveness of an army is "the product of a mass multiplied by something else; by an unknown X...the spirit of the army." A more realistic assessment made when Germany invaded Russia: "the German's came to play tennis, the game was actually rugby".

German WWII Military Service and Casualties

The numbers below were reliably acquired up till November 1944. From that date on, the reporting systems tended to break down. In general terms, it is known that 80 percent of German military deaths took place in the last 2 years of the war. That three quarters occurred on the East front where, as an example, 180,310 died in January 1943 at Stalingrad in that one month alone. In an effort to soften the blow of deaths reported from the East front, emphasis was placed on reporting 'MIA' (missing in action) when possible.

	Served	KIA & MIA	%
Heer / Army	13.6 M	4.2 M	31
Luftwaffe	2.5 M	.433M	17.3
Kriegsmarine	1.2 M	.138M	11.5
W-SS	.9 M	.314M	34.9

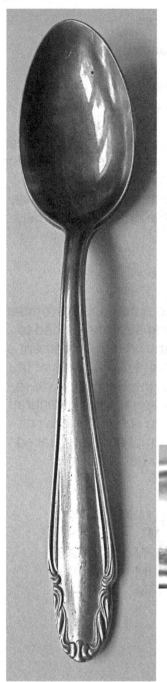

W-64
L = 141 mm / 5 9/16"

W-64 Wehrmacht Eagle

Teaspoon. The eagle (Reichsadler) on this teaspoon's reverse faces to its right (a State organization) over '1942' with maker mark of the Manufacturer's name 'Mangasil' of Solingen with trade mark.

The National Emblem - (Hoheitsabzeichen) was the eagle and swastika of the NSDAP and later Nazi Germany.

Regarding the German Eagle: Per Wikipedia, "The Nazi party used the traditional German eagle, standing atop of a swastika inside a wreath of oak leaves, When the eagle is looking to its left shoulder, it symbolizes the Nazi party and was called the Parteiadler. In contrast, when the eagle is looking to its right shoulder, it symbolizes the country / state / military (Reich) and was called the Reichsadler." After the Nazi party came to power in Germany, they forced the replacement of the traditional version of the German eagle with their modified party symbol highlighting the swastika throughout the country and all its institutions.

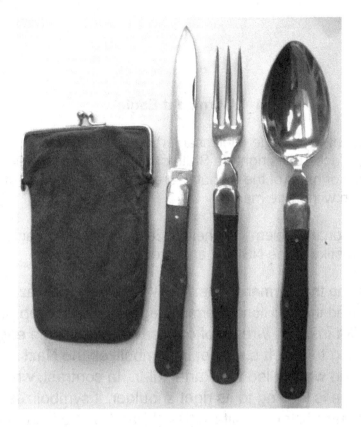

W-65

W-65 OFFICER'S FIELD BESTECK

This matched set of a foldable knife, fork and spoon is from J. A. Henckels and is typical of those used by German Army officers when in the field. The knife is maker marked with the Henckels trademarked 'two stick figures' and impressed with "J.A.Henckels" over "SOLINGEN". When folded, the three pieces fit into a companion buckskin lined leather pouch that snaps shut.

Spoon folded: 112 mm / 4 6/16"
Spoon open: 198 mm / 7 3/4"

Note: Officers Field Besteck: German officers in the field have traditionally shared the enlisted men's food and eaten with the troops. There are many photos of Hitler in the field with the troops and eating with them whereas the British and US have traditionally separated officers from the enlisted men with officers eating their own subsidized, superior rations in private.

W-66

W-66 Army Field Issue Folding Spoon / Fork Combination Cutlery Set (Essbesteck)

This is the standard issue, aluminum construction folding tablespoon and four tine fork combination (spork) and in German a (goffel) gabel und loffel. On the reverse of the spoon handle maker unknown, initials (WSuCL) in a rectangular border. Owners initials, "LB" scratched on the front of the fork between the arrow and the pivotal rivet.

Folded length is 6 inches while opened length is 9 1/2 inches.

Major Early Campaigns

Poland: Invaded 1 Sep 39, ends 6 Oct 39 German losses: 13,111 KIA / MIA and 27,278 WIA vs 800,000 Poles KIA or captured.

Western Campaign begins 10 May 1940, ends 22 June 40: German losses: 27,074 KIA, MIA 18,383 and WIA 111,034. Allies lost 90,000 KIA, 200,000 WIA, 1.9 M captured or MIA

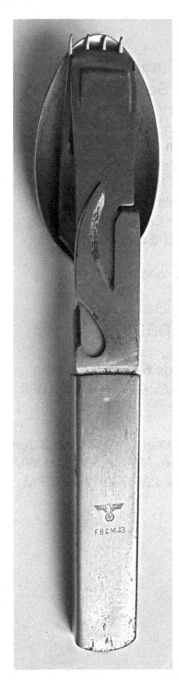

W-67

W-67 Field Issue Cutlery Set (essbesteck)

The set is composed of a knife (195 mm / 7 3/4"), a four tined fork (193 mm / 7 5/8")and a tablespoon(195 mm / 7 3/4"), each of which slide into the slotted handle of a can opener (155 mm / 6 1/8"). The opener is stamped on its solid side with a spread-winged eagle clutching a wreathed mobile swastika in its talons, below which is stamped "FBCM43" all other components are similarly marked with the exception of the unmarked knife. An indentation is along the side of the knife handle which mates with a right angled hook to the top of the can opener. Made in 1943, the basic material is steel with a coating, possibly zinc. The coating has broken down in places and corrosion has occurred. The 1942 models were still made of stainless steel. See M-139

W-68
L = 212 mm / 8 6/16"

W-68 HEER (Army)

Mess Hall Tablespoon (Kantine Esloffel) Roughly 8 3/8"
long, natural aluminum alloy. Handle obverse is flat. The
reverse of the handle is well marked with an impressed
national eagle with outstretched wings and the
manufacturers initials "W.S.M." and dated "42".

> Fact: Of the 13,600,000+ that served in the German
> army from 1939 to 1945, some 4,200,000+ were killed
> or missing in action. Total German losses in the
> Eastern Campaign from 1941 to 1944 alone were
> 1,400,000+ killed in action with an additional 1 million
> missing in action.

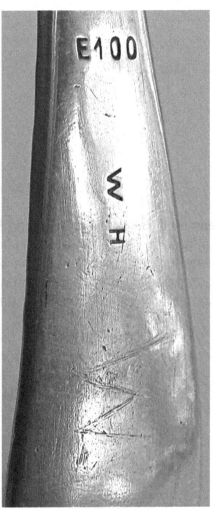

W-69
L = 210 mm / 8 1/4"

W-69 HEER

Mess Hall Tablespoon, Aluminum with raised central rib on obverse. Reverse handle maker marked "E100" and "WH" indicating Wehrmacht (Armed Forces), Heer, (Army). Plus an owner's? initial "W" scratched on reverse.

Trivia: To appreciate the pre 1943 logistics of a German Infantry Division, per "*The German Infantry Handbook*' by Alex Bucher - the 12th Infantry Division in the Eastern campaign from 22 June to 31 Dec 1941, a strengthened division of 20,000 men and 5,500 horses consumed 8,110 tons of food and fodder plus 15,100,000 cigarettes, 98,000 liters of alcohol, 6,516 kilo of chocolate etc. The eastern campaign started with 99 Infantry Divisions and quickly built up to 119!

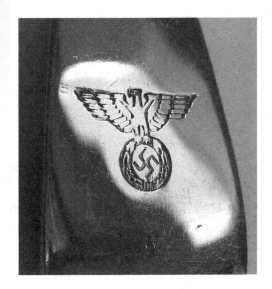

W-70
L = 209 mm / 8 1/4"

W-70 HEER

Tablespoon. Mil Issue, aluminum 8 1/4" long. The obverse of
the handle has a raised central rib while the reverse carries
a manufacturers mark "LGK&F" over 39 and the eagle.

Trivia: Due to manpower shortages and a scarcity of
reserves, by the Spring of 1942, German forces in the
East had 'absorbed' some 800,000 former Red Army
soldiers, including an estimated 6,000 officers and
former commissars. Ultimately, more than one million
former Red Army soldiers would serve with the
Germans. These Soviet citizens that volunteered to be
unofficially employed as manual laborers and/or as
German Army combat reinforcements were called
HiWis for Hilfswillige "volunteer auxiliary" and within the
operational military totaled some 250,000 in 1943 and
were officially permitted to the level of 15% of divisional
strength.   In the East: as of Oct 1943 the German
Infantry Division of 16,860 was reduced to 11,317
Germans and 1,455 HiWi's, a reduction of 28%. In Dec
1944 a further reduction was made to 11,211 Germans
and 698 HiWi's. The HIWI's suffered some 215,000
killed for a death rate of over 25%.

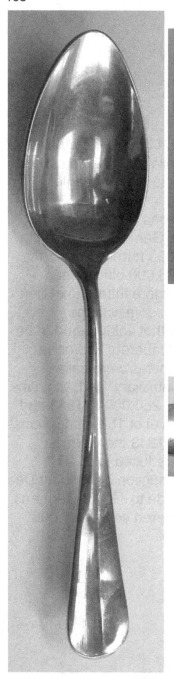

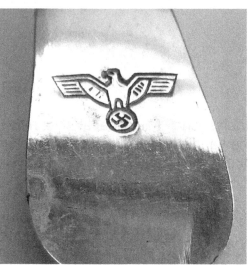

W-71
L = 139 mm / 5 1/2"

W-71 HEER

Demitasse spoon. Alloy with a central raised spine on the obverse and maker marked "B.A.F. N. 39" with eagle facing right on a mobile swastika on the reverse side.

Fact: WWII Campaigns length: Poland 27 Days, Denmark 1 Day, Norway 23 Days, Holland 5 Days, Belgium 18 Day, France 39 Days, Yugoslavia 12 Days, Greece 21 Days.

Blitzkreig? German Infantry Divisions typically relied on their 5,000+ horses to supply 80% of their motive power. Consuming 22 pounds of fodder daily, required some 55 tons of fodder daily per division. For the Polish campaign, the 197,000 horses required 135 railway trucks of fodder daily. Of the 3 million horses and mules enlisted by the German Army between 1939 and 1945, more than 1.7 million perished. These numbers do not include the smaller Panje horses of the East which were used in large numbers but were not officially recognized by the military.

In Leon Degrelle's book, 'Campaign in Russia' he describes an incident in 1942 in the Poltava area where two Cossack cavalry divisions surrendered but only after killing their 12,000 horses so as not to let them fall into German hands.

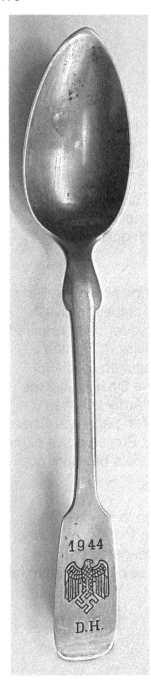

W-72
L = 142 mm / 5 10/16"

W-72 HEER?

Teaspoon. **1944** over **Eagle** looking to his left over **D.H.**
(Deutsches Heer - German Army).   Marked with RM, 800,
'N' (Possibly Ludwig Neresheimer, Hanau, founded 1890)

Although marked with the D.H., the eagle is a Partei eagle
(looking left), that, with the 1944 date would indicate some
type of award or commemorative, possibly to an Army
veteran working in the Partei organization. Dated cutlery
tends to disappear by 1943 when "Advancing on All Fronts"
was a bitter memory as Germany had suffered some
1,686,000 casualties the year before.

Also in 1943, with the fall of Italy, the Germans appropriated
large stockpiles of Italian clothing materials including field
grey Italian material. As a result, the 1943 winter German
army overcoats were mostly made from that Italian field grey
material.

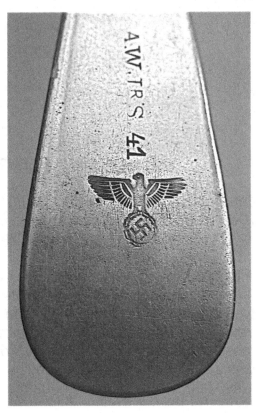

W-73
L = 202 mm / 8"

W-73 Heer

Tablespoon: Obverse unmarked with raised spine, reverse carries A.W.JRS 41

War in the East!

Germany invaded Poland 1 Sep 1939 with 53 divisions (6 armored and 4 motorized). The Western Front had 33 divisions behind the Siegfried Line (West Wall) short of manpower, heavy equipment, artillery and not fully trained. Only 11 divisions were considered fully efficient. France had some 70 divisions facing the Germans. Hitler was surprised when England and France declared war but was confident they would do nothing. In the event, France killed some 200 german soldiers and retired to the Maginot Line. England's philosophy was they could starve Germany into submission by sea control as they had done in WWI.

Germany's surprise attack on The Soviet Union started on 22 June 1941 (Napoleon invaded on 24 June) with 3.2 M soldiers, 2,000 aircraft, 3,350 tanks, 7,184 pieces of artillery 750,000 horses and 20,000 vehicles of some 2,000 types scoured from all over the occupied countries as well as Germany. Advanced 350 miles in 10 days, Started the Leningrad siege on 8 Sept 41, took Minsk in August and Kiev in Sept, Reached Moscow suburbs in December. By the end of 1941, almost 1M Soviet jews had been murdered, all before the Wannsee Conference of Jan 42. The East front exceeded 1000 miles in depth with a length of 2,500 miles! It was here that the major strategic weaknesses of the German military became obvious as contributing factors in its failure. The three failed areas were intelligence, personnel and logistics.

174

W-74
L = 207 mm / 8 2/16"

W-74 Heer

Table fork:. Obverse clear with a raised center spine.
Reverse still carries the German Empire eagle (as this fork
was undoubtedly contracted for in 1933) over 'H.U.'and over
"1934". The H.U.is short form for Heeres Unterkunft (Army
Quarters / Billets). Unidentified maker mark of a shield with
an 'A' above, a 'B' to the left and an 'F' to the right followed
by 'alpaca'

By 1937, preparations for the German economy for the
forthcoming war had been worked out in amazing detail.
Recognizing that wartime controls, to be effective, must be
based on adequate information, comprehensive surveys of
180,000 industrial plants in Germany had compiled statistics
concerning the composition of the labor force as to sex, age,
and training, the consumption of raw and auxiliary material,
fuels, power, the productive capacity, the domestic and
foreign trade as well as the supply of material and products
in the beginning and at the end of the year.

In parallel, 80 million ration cards had already been printed
and deposited with the Landrat's, Chief Mayors, and
corresponding authorities. The further distribution of the
ration cards to the individual households was to be prepared
by these authorities to take place within 24 hours after
mobilization has been ordered.

The needs of the Armed Forces and the civilian minimum
needs in wartime were compared with the covering thereof
by supplies and production.

W-75
L = 240 mm / 9 7/16"

W-75 Heer

Mess Hall Knife: Marked with "H. U. 38 " on the reverse. H.U. is the short form for Heeres Unterkunft (Army Quarters / Billets) 1938.

n 1933 Germany had a 100,000 man Military as prescribed by the Treaty of Versailles in 1920. The Wehrmacht (Armed Forces) was founded on 15Mar35 and the German military was expanded to 3,180,000 in 5 years under Hitler.

The Wehrmacht on 1Sep39 had 3,180,000, (with 2.7 Million heer/army). Maximum strength achieved was 9.5 Million under arms with 5.5 Million in the Heer and at 9 May 1945 some 7.8 Million were still under arms with 5.3 Million Heer. Heer typically accounted for 75% of the Wehrmacht and within the Heer, 82% were Infantry Divisions.

W–76
L = 153 mm / 6"

179

W-76 Heer

Mess Hall Spoon: Marked with "H. U. " on the obverse.
H.U. is the short form for Heeres Unterkunft (Army Quarters /
Billets) This spoon appears to be a 'dug' item with heavy
corrosion but carries the Heer eagle looking right with no
makers mark. The material is undetermined but indicates a
late war product as does the workmanship.

Now we have H.U. utensils from 1934, 1938 and most
probably 1944/45. It is interesting to see how fast Germany
was able to prepare the military for the anticipated
aggressive war aims of Hitler.

Military Spending in the 3rd Reich in billions of Reichsmarks
(2.5 RM = $1) leading up the the War and increasing the
National debt by 300% was:

1Jul/-30Jun	RM-B	Wehrmacht
1932		100,000
33/34	.75	
34/35	4.09	240,000
35/36	5.49	300,000
36/37	10.27	
27/38	10.96	
38/39	17.25	
1Sept1939		3,180,000
		Heer = 2.7M

Compare this spoon with the tableware of the elite Fuhrer
Begleit Brigade W-74.

W–77
L = 212 mm / 8 5/16"

W-77 89th Infantry Regiment's, 5th Company
(Prize for extraordinary shooting skill)

Tablespoon: This award to "Feldwebel Ostrowsky 5./89" dated 22/10/38 is on a spoon from the original officer's club of the 89th Mecklenburg Infantry Regiment which fought in both the Franco-Prussian War and WWI and was disbanded in 1919. Reverse Maker Marked with Wellner's "GOWE", 800, RM.

A new 12th division was secretly formed in 1934 and recognized with the creation of Wehrmacht in 1935. Initially, the division included Infantry Regiments 27 & 48. In 1937, Infantry Regiment 89, raised in Schwerin (Mecklenburg's capital) was added. An Infantry Regiment was composed of 3 Battalions, each with 4 companies, (3 rifle and 1 machine gun). In 1939 it fought in Poland and in 1940 it participated in the invasion of France. It was on occupation duties until May 1941, in the Netherlands. In June 1941 the division joined Operation Barbarossa under Army Group North, and remained under that command until the end of 1943. In 1942 it was one of the divisions encircled in the Demyansk Pocket. In December 1942, it was renamed Grenadier Regiment 89. At the beginning of 1944 the division was transferred to Fourth Army, under Army Group Center; in June, it was one of those facing the Soviet offensive in the Belorussian SSR, It was ordered to hold Mogilevat at all costs, and was destroyed there. Very few troops escaped back to German lines from the encirclement. Thus disappeared the 89th Regiment and its 5th Company.

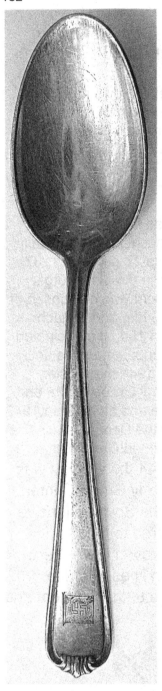

W-78
L = 138 mm / 5 7/16"

W-78 Fuhrer Begleit Brigade, Heer

Teaspoon. Fuhrer Begleit Brigade (FBB:Fuhrer Escort Brigade) Obverse bears the mark of the "Fuhrerstandarte" the Reichskanzlers personal flag with the four corner eagles and a wreathed swastika in its center. The reverse marked: BSF (Bremer Silberwarenfabrick, Bremen) 90. The spoon is from the mess hall dining sets most likely from their garrison H.Q. in Fallsingbostel next to Hitler's (Wolf's lair) at Rastenberg, East Prussia where they were responsible for guarding the outer perimeter of the headquarters, The SS being responsible for protection inside the perimeter.

After the 1 September 1939 attack on Poland, Hitler put Rommel in charge of a new Army battalion being organized to function as his personal escort to the front in the absence of the Leibstandarte. This led to the Führer Begleit Battalion (FBB). The FBB started accompanying Hitler on his train (OG-117) and on his battlefield tours following the Battle of France, and later was upgraded to Division.

Note: Otto Remer commanding this elite unit was the man who almost single handed as an "Oberst" (Major) with his loyal troops were ultimately responsible of completely foiling the July 20th 1944 assassination plot against Hitler. If you see the film Valkyrie (Walkurie) he was the officer who upon orders from the Wehrmacht High Command was sent to arrest Doctor Goebbels, but after the Doctor handed him the phone, he heard on the other end, "Hello Oberst Remer- Do you know who I am? Do you recognize my voice?" It was then that Remer knew that Hitler was alive and he now knew who needed to be apprehended. In the movie, it is he who walks up to all the assembled big wigs including General Beck and announces, "You are all under arrest for high treason!". Remer ultimately rose to the rank of Major General.

W-79
L= 144 mm / 5 11/16"

W-79 First Mountain Division, Heer

Teaspoon. Obverse with edelweiss and reverse RM, 800, HTB (Hanseatishe Silberwarenfabrik, Bremen

The 1.Gebirgsjäger-Division was formed on April 9th, 1938 in Garmisch Partenkirchen from the original Gebirgs-Brigade, the sole mountain unit of the German military since 1935 when the Wehrmacht was formed. After WWI ended, because of their record in battle, the Weimar Republic kept a small cadre of mountain troops to use as the nucleus for a future mountain force. In 1935 this cadre of men helped form the basis of the Gebirgs-Brigade, and by April of 1938, it was raised to a Divisional unit, the 1.Gebrigs-Division.

Campaigns: Poland 1939. Western 1940: After the Campaign in France, the Division was posted to take part in the planned invasion of Great Britain, and then for the planned invasion of Gibraltar, but in both cases, the planned operations were canceled. Balkans 1941: After training for the above two invasions, the Division was transferred to Austria to take part in operations in Yugoslavia. On April 9th, 1941, two years after the Division was formed, it crossed the Yugoslav frontier and fought through central Yugoslavia with the bulk of the German forces. Eastern Front: 1941-1943 After the Campaigns in Yugoslavia, the Division took part in the Invasion of the Soviet Union and fought in the highest positions held by any unit in all of German military history when the 4300 meter (14,100 ft) heights of Mt. Elbrus in the deep Caucasus region was held by the Gebirgsjäger against repeated Soviet attacks and the harsh high alpine elements. Balkan/Italian Fronts: 1943-1945 In December, 1944 the Division was again moved to Hungary where it took part in offensives against the Red Army, and was then moved to the Austrian Region in 1945 where it surrendered to the Americans in May of 1945.

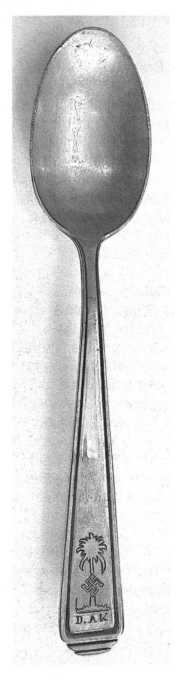

W-80
L =145 mm / 5 11/16"

W-80 D.AK,
das Deutsches Afrikakorps
(The German Africa Corps)

Teaspoon. Marked with DAK logo with maker mark 'AWS' in a squared box (August Wellner & Sohne), The AWS maker mark was used by Wellner from 1928 to 1941, 800, RM.

The D.AK was formed on 12 Feb 1941 as the original German expeditionary force in Libya. Tunisia and Egypt during the North African Campaign of World War II. Its original mission was to act as a blocking force in Libya and Tunisia to support the routed Italian army group which was under great pressure by the British forces.

 The force was kept as a distinct formation and became the main German contribution to Panzer Army Africa which evolved into the German-Italian Panzer Army (Deutsch-Italienische Panzerarmee) and Army Group Africa

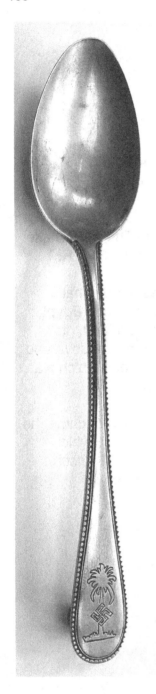

W-81
L = 144 mm / 5 11/16"

W-81 D.AK,

Teaspoon. das Deutsches Afrikakorps marked with D.AK logo. Small dots surround the top handle of the spoon. Maker marked C.A. Krall, 800, RM.

Rommel's AfrikaKorps required 70,000 tons of material monthly to operate but typically received much less. On 13 May 1943 the remnants of the Afrikakorps surrendered in Tunisia having suffered some 12,808 killed in action. By this time, due to the absence of German supplies, the D.AK transport vehicles were predominately made up of captured British trucks.

W-82
L = 118 mm / 4 5/8"

W-82 German Africa Corps

Teaspoon. Obverse DAK logo, Reverse: 800, no RM, the Danish "Three Tower Mark" with year '53' (1853) and Assay Master mark of Peter R. Hinnerup served from 1840 to 1863. The Danish cutlery was undoubtedly confiscated after occupation. The German '800' over stamped later.

The Afrika Korps was derived and formed upon Adolf Hitler's personal choice of Erwin Rommel to its command on February 12, 1941 (Rommel himself landed on African soil in Libya on February 14, 1941 to begin leading his forces that would be brought into action). The German Armed Forces High Command or Oberkommando der Wehrmacht (OKW) and Army High Command or Oberkommando des Heeres (OKH) had decided to send a "blocking force" or Sperrverband to Libya to support the Italian army. On August 15, 1941, the German 5th Light Division5./ leichte "AFRIKA" Division was re designated 21st Panzer Division (commonly written as 21./PD), On February 23, 1943 Panzer Army Africa, (now called the German-Italian Panzer Army,) was re designated as the Italian 1st Army and put under the command of Italian general Giovanni Messe, while Rommel was placed in command of a new Army Group Africa (Heeresgruppe Afrika), created to control both the Italian 1st Army and the 5th Panzer Army. The remnants of the Afrikakorps and other surviving units of the 1st Italian Army retreated into Tunisia. Command of the Army Group was turned over to von Arnim in March. On May 13, remnants of the Afrikakorps surrendered, along with all other remaining Axis forces in North Africa.

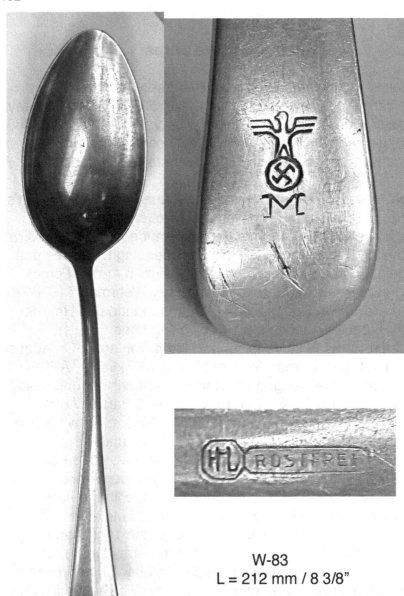

W-83
L = 212 mm / 8 3/8"

W-83 KREIGSMARINE (KM)

Tablespoon. (Navy) Mil Issue, stainless steel with raised spine on obverse. On the reverse the manufacturers initials, 'HHL' for (Heinrich Haupt Ludenscheid Besteckfabrik) in an octagonal border, "ROSTFREI' with KM logo of a minimal / simplified eagle over a mobile swastika in a circle over the 'M'.

Fact: From the Versailles Treaty strength limitation of 15,000 personnel, over 1,500,000 served in the KM, with some 65,000 killed in action

Note: The Navy appears to be the least interested in the incorporation of the Nazi symbols and their renderings show it.

W-84
L = 144 mm / 5 11/16"

W-84 KREIGSMARINE

Teaspoon. (Navy) Mil Issue with raised spine on obverse. On the reverse the makers mark is a circle divided diagonally by crossed swords with a letter 'V' at the top, letter 'D' on the left and a letter 'N' on the right with a letter 'S' at the bottom, the maker mark for (Vereinigte Deutsche Nickelwerke AG Schwerte) followed by 'BLANCADUR'* and at the bottom of the spoon the Kriegsmarine symbol with the 'M' in bold double outline.

*Blancadur identifies the Blancadur Process of the electrolytic deposition of pure rhodium to achieve a brilliant extremely bright and glossy surface layer.

W-85
L = 211 mm / 8 5/16"

W-85 Kriegsmarine

Tablespoon Kreigsmarine. Obverse of the handle is
unmarked with a low, central ridge. Reverse maker marked
F.W.W. 41. Impressed Kreigsmarine eagle with 3 feathers
but no 'M', Rustfrei.

"The U-Boat Commander's Handbook, New Edition
1943" was translated by the US Navy and published by
Thomas Publications in 1989. This handbook was the
bible for the 1,244 German naval officers that served as
U-Boat commanders.

The U-Boat pens at Lorient, France used 250,000 tons
of cement and 17,000 tons of steel and are still in use
by the French navy.

On 4 May 1945 - Messages were sent to all U-Boats to
cease action. On 5 May, the U-835 sank a collier four
miles off Point Judith, Rhode Island and in turn was the
last German U-boat sunk with the loss of all hands.

W-86   KM/Partei Retirement Gift?

Tablespoon. very ornate with obverse carrying a Parteiadler looking left (symbolizing the Nazi Party) over "Kriegsmarine". The reverse carries maker mark: 'Gebr. Friedlander', '800', 'RM' with engraved initials: JJS.   L = 215 mm / 8 7/16".

This spoons conflicted markings on the obverse make it difficult to place or understand. We can hypothesize that it is not official KM ware due to the Partiadler but as it is expensive, it could be a Partei award?

Navy officer careers consisted of four varying grades: High, Elevated, Medium and Low'. Upon promotion or the retirement of High ranking Kriegsmarine officers, it was traditional to be presented with a commemorative set of table ware. This spoon is not typical of that naval tradition as it is Nazi Party generated and is an obvious departure from the official minimal approach to marking tableware by the Kriegsmarine.

Note: The Kriegsmarine can be said to have had three main components between 1935 and 1945, individual naval vessels, naval formations consisting of specific types of ships and a wide variety of ground based units. From these three main components the Kriegsmarine fielded thousands of ships and hundreds of naval formations and ground units. Between 1939 and 1945 over 1.5 million served in the Kriegsmarine. Over 65,000 were killed, over 105,000 went missing and over 210,000 were wounded. Of the 7,361 men awarded the initial grade of the highest German combat honor of WWII, the Knights Cross, 318 were from the Kriegsmarine making up 4% of the total awarded

W-87
L = 206 mm / 8 1/16"

W-87   Luftwaffe

Tablespoon (Esloffel), (Air Force) Mess Hall One piece stainless steel. The obverse of the handle is marked with a faint, impressed early style "droop tailed" Luftwaffe eagle. The reverse of the handle is well marked with impressed manufacturers initials "CH" for (Chromolit) and date "41", followed by "Rostfrei" (Rust Free). At the end of the handle, stamped crosswise are the initials, "Fl.U.V." indicating, Flieger Unterkunft Verwaltung (Flight Barracks Administration)

The Luftwaffe is considered to be a child of the Nazi party. Under the Versailles Treaty of 1919, Part V, Germany was forbidden from having any military air organizations.

The Luftwaffe was officially recognized by Hitler on 9 March 1935 when he called for volunteers to serve in the German Air Force.

Fact: Of the 3,400,000 that served in the Luftwaffe during the period 1935 to 1945, some 165,014 were killed in action including 70,000 aircrew.

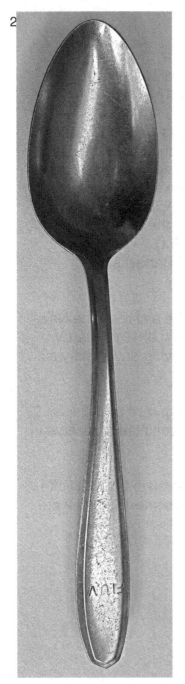

W-88
L = 210 mm / 8 1/4"

W-88 Luftwaffe

Tablespoon, mess hall stainless steel. Obverse of the
handle is well marked with impressed initials "Fl. U.V."
indicating, Flieger Unterkunft Verwaltung, (Flight Barracks
Administration). Manufacturer's name "Oxydex", logo of a 4
leaf clover in a square and "rustfrei" is impressed on the
reverse. The FIUV is impressed upside down.

Luftwaffe Trivia: In 1942, an army study showed that
army strength had peaked and from then on, it would be
unable to make up manpower losses. To make up Heer
losses, Luftwaffe Field Divisions were rapidly mobilized from
Luftwaffe ground personnel. From Oct 42 to early 1943
some 200,000 Luftwaffe personnel were organized into 21
Field Divisions - as 7,000+ strong M1942 Rifle (Jager)
Divisions to replace the massive loss of men on the Eastern
front. Due to the lack of training, poor leadership (the
officers were Luftwaffe) resulted in poor performance in the
field. Of the 21 divisions formed, 17 were either destroyed
or disbanded before the end of the war.

Note: The Army had intended for the 200,000 to be
used to make up Army losses by their integration into
existing army units but Goring successfully opposed
that idea as he did not want his National Socialist
airmen going into the 'reactionary' army. To compound
the army's problem, it had to equip these divisions.

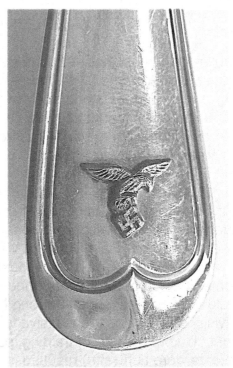

W-89
L = 209 mm / 8 1/4"

W-89 Luftwaffe

Tablespoon with raised, early Droop-Tailed Eagle (1935/6) and swastika on obverse. Maker marked reverse: Roman numeral 'II' which could be an indication that the piece has a double layer of silver plate and a diamond enclosing crossed swords and the letters ''V' at the top of the cross, 'D' on the left, 'N' on the right and 'S' below the cross, the maker mark for (Vereinigte Deutsche Nickelwerke AG Schwerte) Probably silver plate.

Germany's front line fighter plane was the Messerschmitt Bf 109 with direct fuel injection as opposed to the Spitefire's carburetor engine which gave the Messerschmitt significant advantages in certain maneuvers. The kill ratio (almost 9:1) made this plane far superior to any of the other German fighters during the war and over 33,000 were produced. The closest rival was the Focke-Wulf Fw 190 with a kill ratio of 4:1, but introduced later in the war when things were more difficult. Some 20,000 Fw 190's were built. These two aircraft were half the total aircraft manufactured by Germany in WWII.

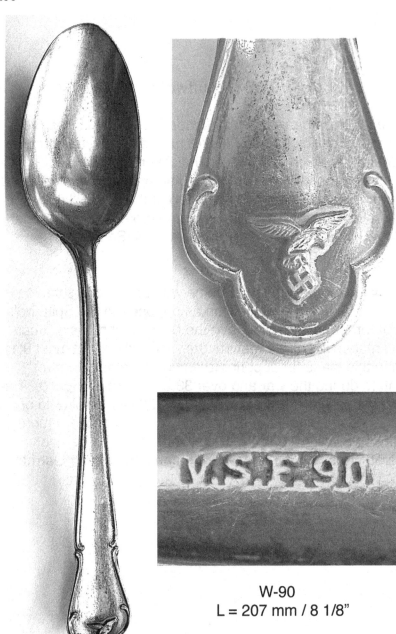

W-90
L = 207 mm / 8 1/8"

206

W-90 Luftwaffe

Tablespoon. Officers Service, in silver plate with raised, early Droop Tailed Eagle and gold plated swastika on obverse. Maker marked on reverse: V.S.F.90

1st Pattern Luftwaffe eagle (1935 & 1936) has the leg positioned horizontally across the eagles body compared to the upward curving leg of the 2nd pattern. Other items of note: 1st pattern's short, stubby wings, and very large swastika.

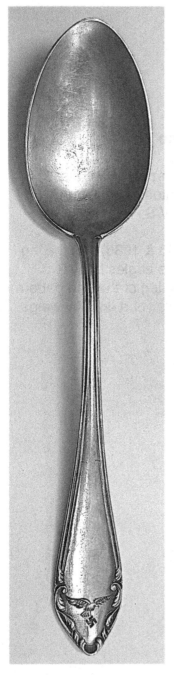

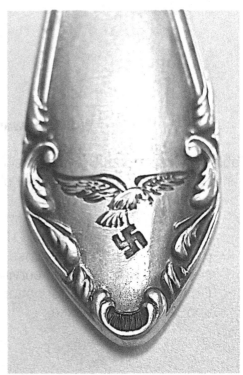

W-91
L = 142 mm / 5 10/16 "

W-91 Luftwaffe

Teaspoon. General Officer's service piece. Marked on obverse with Luftwaffe emblem. Reverse maker mark of Vereinigte Silberwarenfabriken, Dusseldorf, founded 1899 followed by 800, RM.

Maximum air strength in Europe during WWII: Germany 5,000 combat aircraft, America 21,000, England 8,500 and Russia 17,000.

German WWII FIGHTER aircraft production rates:

1939	37/ month.
1940	126/ month
1942	250/ month under Udet
1943	1,000/ month under Milch
Fall 1944	2,500/ month under Speer

Notes: 1. At 5'3", Ernst Udet was Nazi Germany's shortest General. Albert Speer was 6'3".

2. See OG-43, in 1942 the BR-52 Kriegslok (War Locomotives / freight) empty weight 75.9 tons were being built at a rate of 500 per month!

W-92
L = 174 mm / 6 13/16"

W-92 Luftwaffe

Dessert spoon.   General Officers Service in silver with a fraktur personalized? letter "B" over the Luftwaffe Eagle on the obverse. The reverse is well marked with the manufacturer's name 'LAMEYER' followed by the RM of a crescent moon & crown (Halbmond und Krone) and 800 (the decimal silver standard mark) followed by a maker's mark of a small 'W' left of a capital 'L' followed by a '&' and a capital 'S' with a crown on the top. The "W" for the first name of Wilhelm, the 'L' for family name Lameyer, the '& S' most probably for 'and son' of Hanover .

Total German WWII Aircraft production: 113,515 aircraft with 100,000 destroyed and 70,000 aircrew killed.
    (The US produced over 100,000 aircraft in 1944 alone
    of a total 300,000)

    Note: The English teaspoon holds 5 ml, a dessert
              spoon 10 ml and the tablespoon 15 ml.

W-93
L = 152 mm / 6"

W-93 Luftwaffe. Fliegerhorst Julich 1936
(Air Base Julich)

Nut Cracker. One arm: Fl. H.Kdtr.Jü. 1936 (Fliegerhorst Kommandantur Jülich 1936), or Air Base Headquarters Julich 1936. Other arm: first pattern (1935 & 6) eagle with swastika and reverse maker marked WELLNER, 10 and 3

Jülich is a good size German city strategically located near the German border with Holland, Luxembourg and Belgium, and played an important role in the invasion of those countries by Wehrmacht forces in 1940. This is a rare and beautiful example of the standard 6 inch heavy, silver plated nutcracker manufactured during the Third Reich in Aue, Germany by the firm of August Wellner & Sohne and is one of the rarest pieces of Wellner Luftwaffe table service. Founded in 1935, during this early period of the Luftwaffe, German base specific cutlery made its appearance which by itself is rare. The engraving style and time frame is harmonious with W-77 & M-136's Maker Mark. Hermann Göering personally chose an insignia for the Luftwaffe that differed from that of the other armed branches. The eagle, an old symbol of the German Empire, was used, but in a different posture. Since 1933, when Hitler's National Socialist Party came to power, the eagle held between his claws the symbol of the party—the swastika (an old symbol of sunrise) —which usually was enveloped by an oak wreath. Göering rejected the old heraldic eagle because he felt it was too stylized, too static, and too massive; instead he chose a younger, more natural and lighter eagle with wings spread as if in flight, as he considered this a more suitable symbol for an air force. While the Wehrmacht eagle held the symbol of the National Socialist Party firmly in its talons, the Luftwaffe eagle held the swastika with only one talon while the other was bent in a threatening gesture.

214

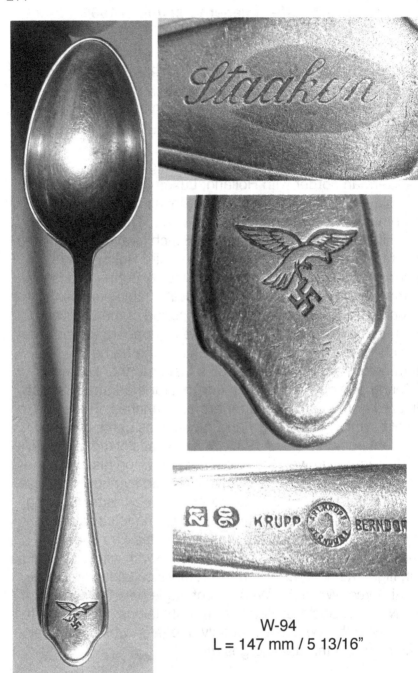

W-94
L = 147 mm / 5 13/16"

215

W-94 Luftwaffe Fliegerhorst "Staaken"
(Air Base Staaken)

Desert Spoon. Obverse marked with a well-detailed, incised, 2nd pattern (1937 - 1945) Luftwaffe eagle and swastika. Reverse: Style "21", Silver "90" and maker mark "Krupp Berndorf" and air base ID "Staaken" in jeweler script.

Staaken is located approximately 17 km west of central Berlin. Here during WWI the Luftschiffbau Zeppelin company manufactured zeppelin airships and R.VI biplane strategic bombers. In 1919 the regulations of the Treaty of Versailles ended zeppelin production and the area was transformed into an airfield. In 1927, the former zeppelin manufacturing halls were locations for various film productions including parts of Fritz Lang's Metropolis (a favorite of Hitler and the most expensive silent film ever produced!). In 1929 the estate was sold to the City of Berlin, while parts of the airport were still used by the Lufthansa airline for flight training and maintenance purposes.

From the founding of the Luftwaffe in 1935 till 1945, this field was the home of Luftwaffe Air Base Staaken (Fliegerhorst Staaken) although it shared the property with the Demag (Deutsche Maschinenfabrik AG) that built Panther tanks during World War II using forced labor of over 2,500 prisoners held in the nearby Falkenhagen labor camp, a sub camp of Sacksenhausen concentration camp.

2nd Pattern eagle (1937 - 45) "Droop Tailed" has a pronounced downward pitch to the tail feathers and the eagles free leg lifts upward in a pronounced curve. Source comment: Spoon shows light surface wear/age with some loss of silver plating to underside of the spoon bowl and adjacent to the Staaken personalization.

Wehrmacht's Military Justice

Oath: From "*The Hitler Salute*' by Tilmer Allert: "Oaths are by their nature unconditional: they are made to ward off the possibility that the intensity of the relationship they govern will slacken and fall prey to moral weakness or negligence."

Until 1933, members of the German military swore their oath of allegiance in the following words: "I swear by God this sacred vow that I will faithfully and truly serve my people and my country at all times, and that I will be prepared as a brave and obedient soldier to be ever willing to risk my life to uphold this vow."

In 1934, the wording was changed to: "I swear by God this sacred vow that I will offer my unqualified obedience to the leader of the German Empire and the German people, Adolf Hitler, the commander-in-chief of the military, and that I will be prepared as a brave soldier to be ever willing to risk my life to uphold this vow."

For comparison

US Military enlistment oath: " I, (NAME), do solemnly swear (or affirm) that I will support and defend the Constitution of the United States against all enemies, foreign and domestic; that I will bear true faith and allegiance to the same; and that I will obey the orders of the President of the United States and the orders of the officers appointed over me, according to regulations and the Uniform Code of Military Justice. So help me God."

Initial problems were created with the basic requirement to take the oath. The Jehovah's Witnesses were the only group of people in German society which refused as a unified body to serve in the armed forces. In addition, after their occupation, the citizens of Luxembourg as well as the French citizens of Alsace and Lorraine were made ethnic German citizens and therefore subject to being drafted by the Wehrmacht. Polish citizens that were classified as ethnic Germans were also subject to the draft. In all these cases, to refuse to take the oath of allegiance to Hitler automatically triggered the death penalty which was administered by the military courts.

The next level of legal enforcement of military discipline occurred after joining the Wehrmacht and having taken the oath. Now the focus is the maintenance of discipline.

Obedience to orders is fundamental to military organization. The individual abandons the right to self determined decisions by joining the armed forces. Unconditional obedience, subordination and military unity is the goal.

Some one million Wehrmacht soldiers were subjected to military courts for failing (wehrkraftzersetzer) "subverting the power of defense". Of these some 20,000 were executed for this offense. (Numbers executed for criminal crimes is not included). For comparison, the US actually executed one soldier in WWII and Germany had executed 48 during WWI.

Example: An enlisted soldier in Poland was ordered to shoot an old woman who refused to surrender her 2 pigs to his forage unit. After refusing 3 direct orders, he was arrested, tried and shot.

SS

An explanation as to the plethora of SS Besteck comes from an item in a Germania International write-up: "Traditionally, in Germany, tableware was the gift of choice. This involved sets of spoons, knives and forks sometimes in special cases. There was born a tradition in the Waffen-SS of presenting table ware to couples who were about to be married. This went back to the 1930's with the Allgemeine-SS. From 1939 on, thousands of war wounded of the Waffen-SS had nothing to do other than lie around in hospital beds or languish about with no actual mental therapy. The SS command decided that various artistic projects should be offered to them that would fill the bill. The question was what therapy would give the recuperating soldier something to occupy his hours, and at the same time be something that would add to the cultural expression and acumen that was always the professed agenda of the SS. Then someone came up with the idea of supplying the men with simple tools for constructing various items such as presentation dinnerware and also engraving tools and applique kits were supplied for acid etching and hand engraving. The men were allowed to sell these hand tooled gifts. One of the most popular of the art projects was making up sets of dinnerware--knives, forks, spoons--with the SS symbols applied. The actual flatware was not produced by these wounded men, rather it was a matter of certain companies who produced these utensils to donate them to the soldiers who, with their newly acquired tools, applied carefully the SS runic symbols to the various pieces. Firms such as Krupp, Sy and Wagner, Tiger, Eickhorn, Wellner etc., donated sets from vendor stocks to be decorated and sold with the benefits going to the soldiers families.

These were often called wedding sets because SS men of various Waffen-SS units would often give them as presents to a comrade and his wife as a marriage present. It became a respected tradition among the ranks of the Waffen-SS and continued on to the end of the war." With over 900,000 serving in the Waffen-SS, and over 400,000 wounded in action, this was a large number to find distractions via the Verwundete (wounded) Program!

Legal Problems for the SS

Due to its creation by Hitler personally and its subsequent involvement with the NSDAP as a Party-affiliated organization, the SS was listed as a criminal organization at Nuremberg in 1945. The Waffen-SS (the militarized formations of the SS were named Waffen-SS in the winter of 1939-40 having originally been formed as the SS-VT or SS (Special Troops) was thus denied the rights of the other military service veterans. Only conscripts sworn in after 1943 were exempted from criminal charges on the basis of involuntary servitude. All Allgemeine-SS members were listed as criminals.

The SS mottos: Meine Ehre Heisst Treue -
My Honor is Loyalty
&
Believe! Obey! Fight!

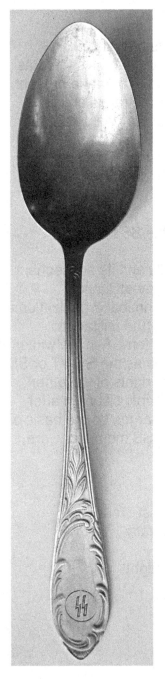

SS-95
L = 211 mm / 8 5/16"

SS-95

Tablespoon. Obverse carries the SS Runes in a circle while the reverse is marked 'NEUSILBER'. Neusilber was created by the Gebrueder Henninger (Henninger Bros.) as a substitute for silver and was composed of 5-30% nickel, 45-70% copper and 8-45% zinc with trace amounts of lead, tin and iron. It later used the trade name Alpacca.

SS Regalia: Adopted as a link to the past, the Totenkopf (Death's Head) was the only common badge of all SS formations such as the Allgemeine-SS and Waffen-SS.

> From a 15th Century poem by Garnier von Susteren:
> Behold the Knight
> in solemn black manner.
> With a skull on his crest
> and blood on his banner

> The Stosstrupp Adolf Hitler adopted the Totenkopf in
> 1923 whose regimental song included:
> In black we are dressed,
> In blood we are drenched,
> Death's Head on our helmets.
> Hurrah! Hurrah!
> We stand unshaken!

The SS Runes was designed by Walter Heck in 1931 by combining two Sig-Runes side by side. The Sig-Rune was a symbol of victory.

An SS motto: "To accept death and to hand out death".

SS-96
L = 202 mm / 7 15/16"

SS-96 Allgemeine SS-F.S. Braunschweig

Fork. Obverse clear, Reverse Marked SS-F.S. SS -F.
(Fuss / Foot / Infantry) S. (Standarte / Standard unit) over
'Braunschweig'. Maker mark 'WMF' (Wurttembergische
Metallwarenfabrik of Geislingen, 1853 to present.
'Cromargan' is a registered trademark of WMF composed of
18% Chrome, 10% Nickel and 72% steel.

This is an Allgemeine-SS fork. Allgemeine translates to
General or Universal.. Hitler assisted Himmler in his first
great victory over the SA by decreeing on November 7,
1930: "The task of the SS is first the practice of the police
service within the party. No SA leader is entitled to give
instructions to the SS!" Its original role was to protect Hitler
then to support the police in maintaining order which later
developed into a force to combat internal uprisings. By the
start of the war The Allgemeine-SS had 485,000 members in
Germany. With the war, only 100,000 were exempted from
military service and by 1945 that number had been reduced
to 48,500.

Braunschweig (Brunswick, Brunswiek) is a city in central
Germany's Lower Saxony. It is the city in which Adolf Hitler
sought and found employment with the Braunschweig State
Government in February 1932 to qualify for German
citizenship (Hitler being Austrian) which was required to
become a candidate for the German Reichstag. This was
his first step to becoming the leader of the state
(Reichskanzler).

Note: The Standarte was originally composed of 2,000,
reduced to 1,000 in 1941 and finally to 400 in 1945. There
were 127 Standarte in November 1944 each associated with
a particular metropolitan area. Braunschweig's Standarte
was designated number 49.

SS-97
L = 145 mm / 5 11/16"

SS-97 Allgemeine-SS Standardt 28, Hamburg

Teaspoon, Obverse marked '28=SS=Standarten'. Reverse
Reichsmark, 800 unknown Maker Mark of a bird in a circle
looking left and 'ARON'.

The Standarten was the standard unit of the Allgemeine-SS /
General SS as set up in 1930 with a nominal goal of 2,000
men. Each SS Stardarte was composed of three active
Sturmbanne or battalions one reserve Sturmbann and a
marching band. The Sturmbann strength was nominally
between 500 and 800 men. Within the Sturmbannn were
four Sturme or companies, a medical squad and a fife and
drum corps. A Sturm nominally had between 120 and 180
men. The Sturm was further divided into 3 or 4 Truppen
(platoons) each composed of 3 Scharen (sections). The
Schar composed of between 10 and 15 men. Standarten
were numbered consecutively from 1 to 127.   Number 28
being located in Hamburg.

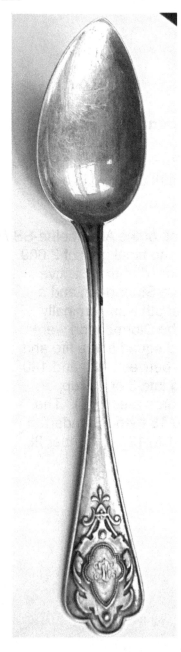

SS-98
L = 208 mm / 8 3/16

227

SS-98 Waffen-SS

Tablespoon, Obverse baroque with engraved owner initials of 'DJC'. Reverse with impressed 'Waffen-SS', RM, 800 and a Bruckmann & Sohne trade mark 'eagle'.

> On 26 July 1934, Adolf Hitler announced that "in consideration of the very meritorious service of the SS, especially in connection with the events of 30th June 1934,(night of the Long Knives when the SA leadership was killed by the SS) I elevate it to the status of an independent organization within the National Socialist Worker's Party."
>
> Originally, Waffen-SS personnel requirements called for a minimum height of 5'11" for all volunteers except for the LAH which required a minimum height of 6'1".
>
> The term 'Waffen-SS' was made official during Feb 1940.
>
> Special note; Although Austria had only 8 percent of the population of Germany, it supplied 14 percent of the SS manpower.

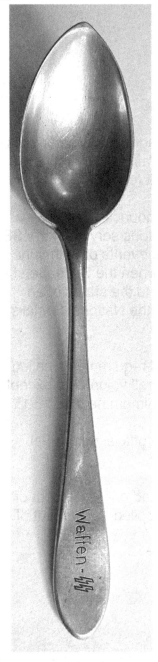

SS-99
L = 149 mm / 5 14/16"

229

SS-99 WAFFEN-SS

Teaspoon. Obverse plain with no decoration marked
'Waffen-SS'. Reverse hallmarked with a Wellner's
'elephant' over 'Alpacca' enclosed in an oval.

Waffen-SS or Armed-SS, literally Weapons-SS was the
combat arm of the Schutzstaffel and founded in 1939.

Waffen-SS consisted of 38 combat divisions, each with
numerical designations followed by such names as "SS
Panzer Division", "SS Panzergrenadier Division" and "Waffen
Grenadier Division Der SS". The 3rd SS Panzer Division =
"Soldiers of Destruction" and the 12th SS Panzer Division =
'Fighters not Soldiers". Waffen-SS KIA estimated at
180,000, WIA 400,000 and MIA 70,000.

> Waffen SS Trivia: Although some 922,000 served in
> the Waffen-SS, ultimately 57 percent were non-German
> nationals! Breakdown: Reich Germans 400,000, West
> Europeans 137,000, East Europeans 200,000 and
> Volksdeutsche (ethnic Germans) 185,000. Initially the
> W-SS was 'German'. In 1940, with the founding of the
> Wiking Divison it became 'Germanic' The so called
> 'Germanic' divisions being the 1st LSSAH, 2nd Das
> Reich, 3rd Totenkopf and the 5th Wiking. From 1941
> on, it became, per Leon Degrelle, the first truly
> European Army, ultimately composed of volunteers
> from 30 countries such as the 54,000 from Rumania
> and the 50,000 Islamic volunteers.

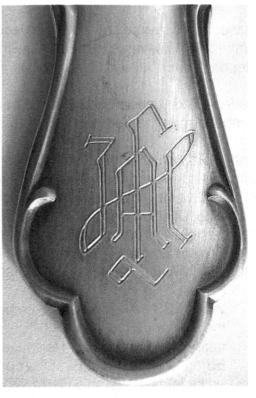

SS-100
L = 208 mm / 8 3/16"

SS-100 1st SS Panzer Division
'Leibstandarte Adolf Hitler'

Tablespoon. **Liebstandarte SS Adolf Hitler.** Obverse carries the formal pattern (also referred to as 'twisted wire' pattern) of intertwined LAH letters as used in the barracks of the SS-Leibstandarte Adolf Hitler, the elite soldiers of the Schutzstaffel, or Black Corps. Reverse maker marked 'V.S.F. 90'.

Raised in September 1933, the original LSSAH compound was located in South West Berlin at the Lichterfelde Kaserne (Berlin-Lichterfelde) which was an old Prussian cadet training school and became the headquarters for Hitler's body guard regiment, the Leibstndarte-SS "Adolf Hitler". Later became the headquarters for the SS-Panzer-Division Leibstandarte under 'Sepp' Dietrich .

The spoon is in the Beidermeier pattern which evolved in such cities a Vienna, Munich and Berlin during the 'Beidermeier' period of 1815 - 1848 in Germany and Austria.

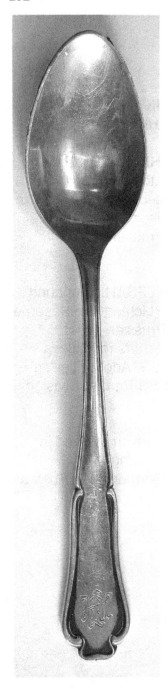

SS-101
L = 144 mm / 5 11/16"

SS-101   LSSAH

Teaspoon. Intertwined script letters L-A-H. Sometimes referred to as twisted wire design. Maker marked "Becker 90".

This premier Waffen-SS Panzer Division was formalized on the 10th anniversary of the Beer Hall Putsch on 8 / 9 November 1933, It was Adolf Hitler's original bodyguard / lifeguard unit, commanded by SS-Gruppenfuhrer Josef 'Sepp' Dietrich. Fought in Poland, Czechoslovakia, Holland, France, Yugoslavia, Greece, Russia, Belgium, and Hungary. Of the June 1944 strength of 19,700 troops, the remaining 1,500 survivors with 16 tanks surrendered to US troops in Austria in 1945.

SS-102
L = 138 mm / 5 7/16"

SS-102 LSSAH 1941

Teaspoon. Obverse marked "LSSAH" 1941. Reverse maker
marked: WMF, (Wurttembergische Metallwarenfabrik of
Geislingen, Germany 1853 to the present), RM, 800.

SS Oath - Nov 33 - "I swear to you, Adolf Hitler, as
Fuhrer and Reich Chancellor, loyalty and bravery. I
vow to you, and those you have appointed to command
me, obedience unto death. So help me God."

In 1929, Hitler described the SS man as, "Those who
throng to the SS are men inclined to the authoritarian
state, who wish to serve and obey, who respond less to
an idea than to a man."

Half of all the W-SS Division commanders (Generals)
died in combat!

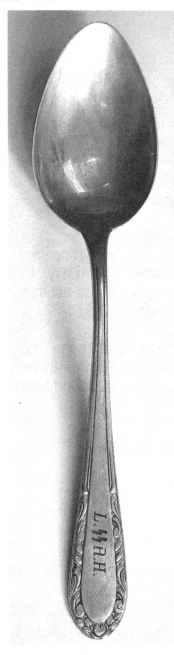

SS-103
L = 136 mm / 5 6/16"

SS-103 LSSAH.

Teaspoon. Obverse monogram: Capital 'L' , 'SS' runes,
Capital 'A' and Capital 'H'. Maker marked on the reverse:
RM, 800, LW in a crest (Lutz & Weiss, Pforzheim founded
1882). Pattern: High relief, floral pattern, both sides,
asymmetrical with roses at base.

In the early years prior to and of WWII, the Army resented
the SS for taking the best candidates (volunteers) and as the
Army controlled procurement for both, they took the best
weapons first, supplying the W-SS with weapons from
acquired / captured stocks.

Weapons fielded to each organization during those early
years:

	Army	W-SS
Pistol	P.08 & P.38	Belgian High Power
Rifle	K98k Mauser	Hungarian 98/40 re-chambered
LMG	MG34 & MG42	Czech ZBvz26

.

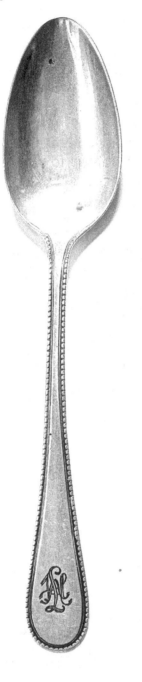

SS-104 L=133 mm / 5 1/4"

SS-104 LSSAH

Teaspoon, Obverse carries the L-A-H intertwined initials. The obverse maker marked by Koch & Bergfeld, Bremen founded 1929, 800 and RM. Also has a hand engraved "G" over "M".

Note: Track 16 of the 2005 digitally re-mastered "Triumph of the Will" DVD of the 1934 Nazi Party Rally in Nuremburg filmed by Leni Riefenstahl has some 5 minutes of the LSSAH review accompanied by their band playing Hitler's favorite, the Badenweiler March with appearances by both Himmler and Sepp Dietrich.

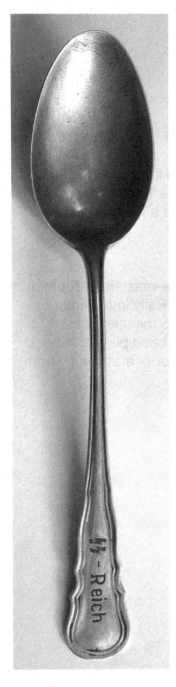

SS-105
L = 140 mm / 5 9/16"

SS-105 SS-Reich

Teaspoon. Obverse monogram SS-Reich, (originally established as the SS-V-Div in October 1939 with later name changes from the April 1940 designation as SS-Division Deutschland to October 1940's 2nd SS-Panzer Division "Reich" and in May 1942, after refitting with more tanks, assault guns and armored personnel carriers it was renamed SS-Panzer Division 'Das Reich'. Maker marked: 800, RM, unreadable entry, XX, for Wilhelm Muller of Berlin. Scalloped handle, double outline.

As a result of the occupation of Czechoslovakia in 1938 - 1939, Hitler was able to detail weapons acquired as: 1,582 airplanes, 2,175 pieces of field artillery, 469 tanks, 500 antiaircraft guns, 43,000 machine guns, 1,090,000 rifles, 114,000 revolvers, a billion rounds of ammunition and 3 million artillery shells in his 28 April 1939 Reichstag speech. Those MG's ended up in the W-SS. See the 3rd SS Panzer Division description SS-110.

242

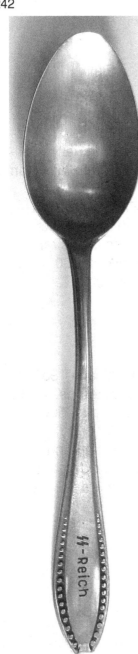

SS-106
L = 139 mm / 5 1/2"

SS-106 SS-Reich

Teaspoon. Obverse SS-Reich. Reverse hallmark: RM, "800", followed by unknown mark with "LSF" in an oblong enclosure. Pattern: bottom 1/ 3rd of obverse has 18 symmetrical dots of increasing size on each side with largest at bottom.

During 1939 and 1940, German forces occupied western European countries which allowed the W-SS to recruit pro-Nazi's, anti communists, Volksdeutsche etc. while the Wehrmacht was not authorized to do so. By the end of 1942, the W-SS fielded some 200,000 troops.

Das Reich received more high bravery / valor awards than any other W-SS Division.

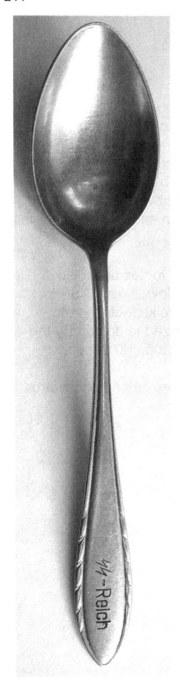

SS-107 L = 146 mm / 5 3/4 "

SS-107 SS-Reich

Teaspoon. Obverse 'SS-Reich' with the SS in what is termed 'lightning bolt' style. Highlights on edges of lower 1/3. Reverse maker marked; Berndorf over their symbol of a 'walking bear' and Alpacca below in an overall oval shape.

SS enlistment requirements were 25 years for officers, 12 years for NCO's and 4 years for enlisted men. The Officer and NCO enlistment durations date from those specified by the Treaty of Versailles for the German Army in an effort to discourage enlistments.

Note: Control of SS mess hall supplies and rations was under SS-WVHA, SS-Wirtschafts und Verwaltungs Hauptamt (SS-Economic and Administration Department.

SS-108
L = 138 mm / 5 7/16"

SS-108 SS-Reich

Teaspoon, Obverse carries a textured SS - Reich. Reverse is unmarked.

On 5 Dec 1941, SS-Obergruppenfuhrer (4 Star) Paul Hausser, commanding SS Division 'Reich' came within 16 kilometers of the outskirts of Moscow, Temperature was -36C / -33F.

SS-Oberstgruppenfuhrer Hauser, whose nickname was "Papa Hauser", lost an eye in combat and became famous as 'the SS general with the eye-patch'.

In 1946, Hauser stated. "The guards of the concentration camps and the personnel in the command did not belong to the Waffen-SS." See the 3rd SS-Panzer Div description SS-110.

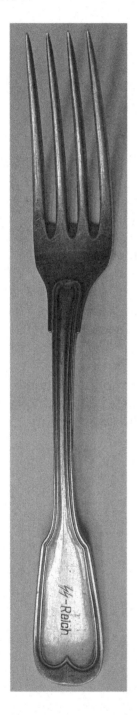

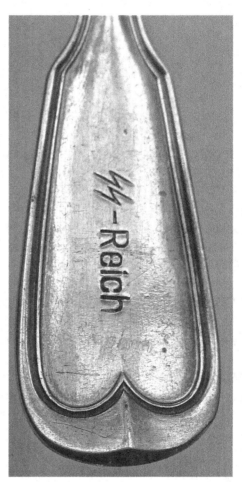

SS-109
L = 103mm / 8 1/16"

SS-109 SS-Reich
(Austria)

Table fork. Obverse carries the 'lightening' SS and Reich. Reverse has an Austrian crowned double headed eagle followed by 'maker mark 'BMF' (Berndorf Metallwaaren Fabrik / Berndorf Metalware Factory) with the M and F sharing the vertical line indicating the plant location as Vienna.

Führer order on the armed units of the SS of 17 Aug 1938 established the SS-VT as political troops at the special disposal of the Nazi regime. Under the Reichsfuhrer-SS for internal security duties, except in time of war when it would be at the disposal of the army.

This translation is from Document 647-PS [translation], in Nazi Conspiracy and Aggression. Volume III: US Government Printing Office, District of Columbia: 1947. pp. 459-466 from the above referenced Fuhrer order:

II. The armed units of the SS
A. The SS-Verfügungstruppe
1. The SS Verfügungstruppe is neither a part of the Wehrmacht nor a part of the police. It is a standing armed unit, exclusively at my disposal. As such, and as a unit of the NSDAP its members are to be selected by the Reichsführer SS according to the ideological and political standards which I have ordered for the NSDAP and for the Schutzstaffeln.

SS-110
L = 141 mm / 5 9/16"

SS-110   3rd SS-Panzer-Division
'Totenkopf' (Death's Head)

Teaspoon. Obverse carries the 3rd's Coat-of-Arms and reverse has the maker mark: E. Kludas, 800, RM.

Raised Nov 1939 with most of the initial enlisted men coming from the SS-Totenkopfverbande, (SS Concentration Camp Guards). Through the Battle of France the division was generally equipped with ex-Czech weapons. In November 1942, 'Das Reich', 'Totenkoph' and 'Wiking' were officially re-designated as SS-Panzergrenadier Divisions, and finally acquired the same type and quantity of equipment to that of army panzer divisions. Surrendered to US troops in Austria 9 May 1945 with less than 1,000 men and 6 tanks from an original strength of 19,000. Handed over to the Russians

Note: Commanded by Theodor Eicke from 14Nov1939 till his KIA on 16Feb943,(shot down behind Russian lines on a recognizance). The 3rd Panzer acquired the identity as "that lost lot" or the Bones Companies. Under Eicke, 'Totenkopf' Div had 60,000 KIA/WIA/MIA vs 'Wiking' Div's 19,000, (the divisions mostly served side by side), the difference is attributed to the commanders. Eicke's favorite guidance: "There is only one thing that is valid, orders!'" and "Tolerance is a sign of weakness".   Totenkopf had the most requests for "transfers out" of any W-SS Division and supplied most of the volunteers for the SS paratroop battalion, generally recognized as a suicide squad.

Note: Eicke, a "dangerous lunatic" imprisoned as a violent hardened criminal was released from a mental hospital in 1933. He personally shot Ernst Rohm on 2July1934, In 1936 he styled himself, (Commander of Death's Head Units or "Fuhrer der Totenkopfverbande") after they were allowed to wear the death's head collar patches.

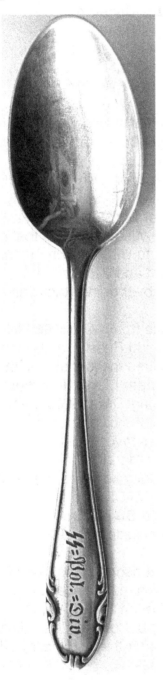

SS-111
L = 141 mm / 5 9/16"

SS-111 4th SS-Panzer Grenadier Division "Polizei"

Spoon. Obverse 'SS=Pol.=Div." and reverse maker marked 800, Reichsmark and 'Siberce'.

This Division was formed and composed of members of the Ordnungpolizei (OrPo / Order Police), the uniformed police on 1 October, 1939 and was not considered to be an elite SS Division because of the manner in which the members of the unit were allowed to join, resulting in the wearing of the Ordnungpolizei uniform with a Heer Eagle on the arm. At the time, SS uniforms were not provided for the unit.

The Division's first action was during the Campaign in France. In 1941, the Division was transferred to the Eastern Front and during heavy fighting for the Luga bridgehead, held by a number of Soviet Divisions, the 4th SS Division lost over 2000 soldiers in bloody frontal assaults but managed to fight into the Northern edge of Luga and encircle and destroy the Soviet defenders.

It was not transferred to the Waffen-SS until 10 February 1942 , when the Division was given "official" Waffen SS status, and in June 1943 its title was changed to 4th SS Panzer Grenadier Division "Polizei" and was sent to the Balkans area. Elements of the Division saw action in Greece on anti-partisan duties and also fought near Belgrade. In January 1945, the Division was pushed into Slovakia, soon after, the 4th SS was moved to Danzig where it was trapped by Soviet forces. After dire battle the Division was shipped across the Hela Peninsula and over sea to Swinemude. There, the Division rested and on 8 May 1945, surrendered to the Russians although some members, attached to Army Group Steiner, surrendered to the Americans.

SS-112
L = 215 mm / 8 7/16"

SS-112 5th SS-Panzer-Division 'Wiking'

Tablespoon. Obverse is flat and unmarked. Reverse carries 'SS-Div. Wiking' & 'ROSTFREI'.

SS-Div. Wiking'. The 5th SS-Panzer-Division (Viking) was originally formed in November 1940 as the SS-Division (mot.) Germania by consolidating the regiments Germania, Nordland (Scandinavians), Westland (Dutch, Flemings) and the 5th SS-artillerie regiment into a new divisional unit. On January 1st 1941 the division was renamed, SS-Division "Wiking" and on November 9th 1942 the division was upgraded and renamed SS-Panzer-Grenadier-Division "Wiking". The division was upgraded again and received its final designation on October 22nd 1943 as 5th SS-Panzer-Division "Wiking" and surrendered in Furstenfeld, Czechoslovakia in May 1945. Although the enlisted men were predominantly Nordic volunteers, it was officered by Germans.

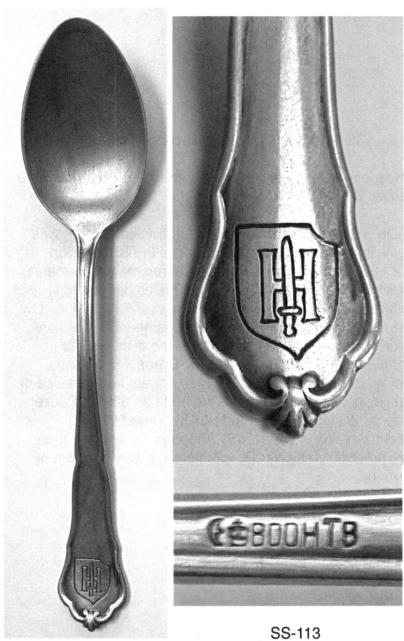

SS-113
L = 133 mm / 5 1/4"

SS-113 9th SS Panzer Division
'Hohenstaufen'

Teaspoon. Obverse carries the 9th's Coat-of-Arms.
Reverse carries the RM, 800 and maker's mark HTB for
Hanseatishe Silberwarenfabrik, Bremen.

The Hohenstaufen, named after the family of the first
German Emperors and specifically for family member
Frederick Barbarossa whom the Fuhrer considered a great
hero. Activated in early 1943 and faced with manpower
shortages, 70 percent of the division's manpower were
conscripts with 60% to 70% from the years 1925/26 or about
18 years of age. Included were a number of ethnic Germans
from Hungary. In June 1944 engaged in Normandy fighting
with a strength of 15,849. By 21 August only 460 men, 20
guns and 23 tanks remained as a result of losses particularly
around Caen and Avranches.. Transferred to Western
Germany in late September to be brought up to strength,
their numbers were made up with Luftwaffe personal and
other remnants. Participated in the failed Ardennes
offensive, moved to Hungary and suffered severe losses
against the Russians in March 1945 west of Budapest.
Hitler was so enraged by their failure to defeat the Russians
that he ordered the men of the 1st, 2nd, 9th and 12th
Divisions of the Waffen SS to be deprived of their
decorations and cuff bands. They fought their way back to
Austria and on 5 May 1945 surrendered to US troops near
Steyr.

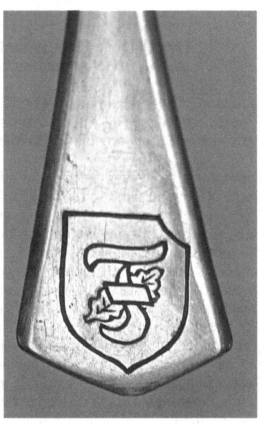

SS-114
L = 138 mm / 5 7/16"

SS-114 10th SS Panzer Division 'Frundsberg'

Teaspoon. The obverse carries the 10th's Coat-of-Arms while the reverse carries 'A. Finster', 800, RM, and the maker's mark of Herman Walter, Halle.

This unit was named after Georg von Frundsberg who lived from 1473 to 1528. Frundsberg was a well known soldier and hero who fought in the services of the Hapsburg Monarchy during several wars.

Recruiting of German conscripts started on 8 January 1943. Reichsführer Heinrich Himmler, when questioned by Adolf Hitler concerning the average age of the soldiers and officers of the division, stated "18 Jahre" (18 years). Division raised in Charente, France and originally named 'Karl der Grosse'.

To the Russian front in March 1944, returned to France June 1944 involved in heavy fighting at Caen, Avranches and Falaise. Moved through Belgium to Arnhem area fighting the British. Moved into Pomeranian on 2 March 1945 and fought heavily in areas Stettin, (Poland) Stargard, Furstenwalde. On 7 May, 1945 remnants of the division destroy 5 Soviet T-34 tanks en-route to Sudetenland. From 10 to 12 May, 1945 the division's remnants attempt unsuccessful reassembly, and disband on their own in an effort to make their way west individually. A number of survivors, who are not captured by either Soviet or Czech forces en-route, surrender to the US 102nd Infantry Division at Tangermünde, on the Elbe River.

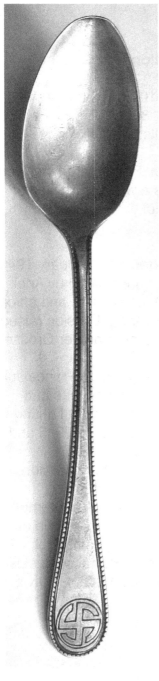

SS-115
L = 145 mm / 5 3/4"

261

SS-115 11th SS-Freiwilligen-
Panzer-Grenadier-Division "Nordland".

Teaspoon. Obverse carries the 11th's Coat-of-Arms.
Reverse is maker marked: G H DANZIGER '800' RM.

Formed in the summer of 1943 of various existing foreign
volunteer units. It was the first SS Division to be officered by
foreign volunteers. Most of the volunteers were from
Scandinavia but the division had the widest range of
nationalities found in a single German division including
Danish, Hungarian, Dutch, Norwegian, Estonian, Finnish,
French, Romanian, Spanish, Swedish, Swiss and British
volunteers that had either served in the division or been
attached to it.   Its emblem is the "Sun wheel" rune - a
circular swastika. On 25 April 1945, the primary defender of
the Reich Chancellery in Berlin was the SS Division
Nordland with virtually no Germans. They had never taken a
prisoner and did not expect to be made prisoners.

   Motto: When all were unfaithful, we remained faithful.

   Note: Along with Nordland, the other W-SS defenders
      of Berlin were the 33rd W-SS Div Charlemagne
      (French) and the 15th W-SS Div (Latvian).

SS-116
L = 133 mm / 5 1/4"

SS-116 12th SS Panzer Division 'Hitlerjugend'

Teaspoon. Obverse with 12th's Coat-of-Arms, reverse 800 RM, maker mark 'FUCHS'

Described as a "crack" division, the Hitlerjugend was unique because the majority of its junior enlisted men were drawn from members of the Hitler Youth born in 1926, (age 17) while the senior NCOs and officers were generally supplied by the 1st SS Panzer Division. They were referred to as the "candy soldiers" as they were too young for normal military rations of spirits and tobacco. The Division insignia depicts the Hitlerjugend sigrune crossing the key of the 1st SS Panzer Division LSSAH's insignia.

The idea of a Waffen-SS division composed of Hitlerjugend (HJ) members was proposed in January 1943. Himmler soon became an enthusiastic advocate as did Hitler, and on 13 February 1943, the official order for the creation was issued.

The division, with 20,540 personnel, first saw action on 7 June 1944 as part of the German defense of the Caen area during the Normandy campaign and it came out of the Falaise pocket with a divisional strength of 12,500 men. In 1944, its commander Kurt "Panzer" Meyer became the youngest general ever to serve in the German military at age 34. On 16 December 1944, the division was committed against the US Army in the Battle of the Bulge, suffering 60% casualties in the 4 week period. After the failure of the Ardennes offensive the division was sent east to fight the Red Army near Budapest. The Division eventually withdrew into Austria and on 8 May 1945, the surviving 7,500 men surrendered to the US Army at Enns.

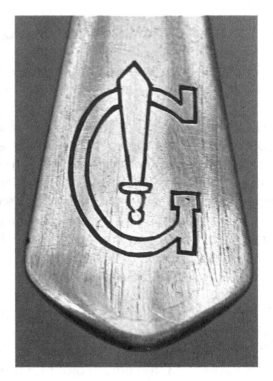

SS-117
L = 125 mm / 4 15/16"

SS-117 Regt; Gruppe 13. SS-Gebirgs 'Handschar'.

Teaspoon. The obverse carries the Regt. Gruppe 13's Coat-of-Arms while the reverse: 800, RM and maker mark of Vereinigte Silberwarenfabriken, Dusseldorf, 1899 -

In the Fall of 1942, SS Reichsfuhrer Heinrich Himmler and SS-General Gottlob Berger approach Hitler with the proposal to raise a Bosnian Muslim SS division. Himmler thought that Muslim men would make perfect SS soldiers, as Islam "promises them Heaven if they fight and are killed in action." Hitler formally approved the project on 10 February 1943 and SS-Obergruppenführer Arthur Phleps, a Romanian ethnic German commander, was charged with raising the division. The 13th Waffen Mountain Division of the SS Handschar (1st Croatian) was commanded by German officers, and composed of native Germans from Croatia (Volksdeutsche), and Bosniaks, who are Muslims from Bosnia and Herzegovina. It was the largest of both the Muslim-oriented divisions and the SS Divisions with 21,065 men, of whom 10% were Croatians. The division had a Muslim Imam for each battalion and a Mullah per regiment. Handschar (Bosnian/Croatian: Handžar) was the local word for the Turkish scimitar a historical symbol of Bosnia and Islam. The Handschar division was a mountain infantry formation, known by the Germans as "Gebirgsjäger". It was used to conduct operations against Yugoslav's primarily Christian Serb Partisans in the Independent State of Croatia from February to September 1944. Recruitment for the division fell as the war progressed and when rumors spread that the division was going to fight the Soviets, the Muslims deserted in droves and was disbanded in October 1944.

The German Volksdeutsche cadre then formed the SS-Gebirgs 'Handschar' (a regimental Group) fought in Hungary and ultimately surrendered to the British in Austria 5/45.

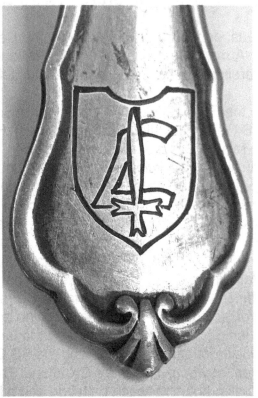

SS-118
L = 142 mm / 5 10/16"

SS-118   37th SS Freiwilligen Kavallerie Division 'Lützow'

Teaspoon. Obverse carries the 37th SS Cavalry Division's Coat-of-Arms. Reverse marked RM, 800, HTB for Hanseatishe Silberwarenfabrik, Bremen.

The 37th SS Volunteer Cavalry Division - Lutzow was listed for the first time on 1March1945. It had been officially established 19Feb1945 following the near-complete annihilation of the 8th and 22nd SS Cavalry Divisions during the Budapest breakout attempt on 11/12 Feb 1945. It consisted of remnants of 8th SS Cavalry Division Florian Geyer and 22nd SS Volunteer Cavalry Division Maria Theresia, including former's SS Pioneer Battalion 8, in addition to mostly 16- or 17-year old German, Hungarian Volkdeutsche, and ethnic Hungarian recruits. The 37th SS also inherited the horses of the two annihilated divisions as both the 8th and 22nd were fighting dismounted when Budapest was surrounded. The new division never exceeded regimental strength. The 37th was the 3rd and last cavalry division of the W-SS. The Division emblem sword was the emblem of the original SS Cavalry Brigade. The division saw action against Soviets as a part of 6th. SS-Panzerarmee during the final weeks of war, before surrendering to Americans in Austria in May.

The Division's namesake, Ludwig Adolf Wilhelm Freiherr von Luetzow (1782-1834) led the swashbuckling German volunteer cavalry unit known as the :Black Troop" in the war against Napoleon in 1813.

Note: 1. A Division motto: "You came very late, still you came".
2. In its last month of existence its strength was reduced from 2,000 to 180.

268

SS-119
L = 204 mm / 8"

AD-149 34th Grenadier Regiment
of the
15th SS Waffen Grenadier Division - 'Latvian No. 1'

Fork. Obverse carries 'CS' for Cesis-Schule. Reverse with
'SS' in a circle, '90' and an unidentified Maker Mark of three
die showing the Four sides, Wellner?

The Latvian city of Cesis was the location of the 34th Gren
Regiment's headquarters. The school building and its
cutlery were used by the 34th during its formation and this
fork had the 'SS' added at that time.

The SS had success in 1942 in recruiting in the Baltic States
forming 'Legions' of "volunteer' units promising German
citizenship, free land and restriction to the war on
Communism. The 15th Waffen-Gren Div der SS was formed
when manpower shortages became obvious after the
invasion of Russia. Latvian conscripts formed the 15th
Waffen-Gren-Div and the "Voluntary" title was dropped when
to increase the unit strength, Himmler enforced compulsory
military service in the Ostland in age groups 1915 to 24 in
1943 and 1904-14 & 1925-26 in 1944.

The 15th fought on the Eastern Front but lost enthusiasm
when their homeland was occupied by the Soviets. The 15th
was decimated in the defense of Pomerania in early 1945.
The survivors participated in the defense of Berlin (see
SS-115). Other remnants surrendered to the Americans at
Gutergluck near the Elbe River.

Note: Some 15,000 Latvians served in the two Latvian SS
Divisions: The 15th SS Grenadier Div. 'Latvian No 1 and
the19th SS Grenadier Div 'Latvian No 2'. All officers were
German.

270

SS-120
L = 142 mm / 5 5/8"

SS-120 39th SS Grenadier Division 'Nibelungen'

Teaspoon. Obverse carries the 39th's Coat-of-Arms.
Reverse has the RM, 800 and maker mark of Gebuder
Reiner, Krumbach Bayern 1910 - present.

The SS-Junkerschule Bad Tölz was the officers training
school for the Waffen-SS. It was the equivalent of the United
States Military Academy. The school was established in
1937, in the town of Bad Tölz which is about 30 miles south
of Munich. The location selected was primarily due to the
beauty of the surrounding area. A sub camp of the Dachau
concentration camp was located in the town of Bad Tölz to
provide labour for the SS-Junkerschule. The 38th SS was
formed on 27 March 1945 from four infantry battalions
mainly composed the staff and students from the school
combined with Himmler's bodyguard battalion and stragglers
from the 30th SS-W Gren Div. It never exceeded a strength
of 6,000 men. The Division was at first named Junkerschule
because of its formation from the members of the SS-
Junkerschule. It was then renamed to Nibelungen from the
medieval poem of the name Nibelungenlied made famous by
Richard Wagner in his opera Ring des Nibelungen. The
original medieval poem and Wagner's opera both revolve
around themes of epic German mythology. The Division
never achieved anywhere near full division status but did see
some combat with its first action in the Landshut area of
Upper Bavaria. The engagement was against American
troops where the 38th over ran a few American positions.
The 38th then saw brief action in the Alpen and Donau areas
before surrendering to the Americans on 8 May 1945 in the
area of the Bavarian Alps.

From 1945 to 1991, the former SS-Junkerschule was the
base of the U.S. Army's 1st Battalion, 10th Special Forces
Group.

272

SS-121
L = 133 mm / 5 1/4"

SS-121   SS.

Teaspoon. A formal pattern in art nouveau style. It is heavily
silver plated approximating the look of real silver.   Reverse
stamped: "P" "100". The SS runes may have been soldered
in place and originally had 14K gold applied which has worn
off in this case. This service is believed to be from the 3rd
SS-Totenkopf Division's Headquarters in the Bavarian
Mountains (SS-Oberbayern).

Trivia: Initially, W-SS Divisions had no Division
chaplain and in 1941 Heinrich Himmler was quoted, "I
have six divisions composed of men absolutely
indifferent in matters of religion. It doesn't prevent them
from going to their deaths with serenity in their souls."
As the composition of the W-SS broadened to that of a
European Army, so did religious tolerance with such
examples as the 28th W-SS Division, Wallonia (French
speaking Belgians) having catholic chaplains and the
13th W-SS Division, Handshar (an Islamic Division)
with both Imams and Mullahs.

Leon Degrelle, CG 'Wallonia' observed that had it not
been for the W-SS and its heroic sacrifices in the East,
the Russians would have arrived in Normandy before
the Allies and all of Europe would have been
communist.

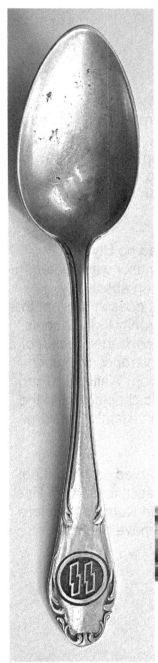

SS-122
L = 142 mm / 5 9/16"

SS-122 SS

Teaspoon. Obverse has the SS in a double circle with scolloped edges Reverse maker marked: E. Kludas, 800 RM. The double circle was also seen on the saddle blankets of the SS equestrians as well as their athletic sport shirts (sporthemd).

> Note: When Germany took over the northern part of Italy on 8 September 1943 as the Italian Social Republic, the SS could then accept Italian volunteers. Himmler forbid them the SS Sigrunen and the SS sleeve eagle. He required them to use Italian specific emblems such as a sleeve eagle clasping a fasces in its talons but they did wear the universal death's head cap emblems.

> Also, with the fall of Italy, the Germans appropriated large stockpiles of Italian clothing materials including camouflage material and the Waffen SS as a result, took a large percentage of that camouflage material for later Waffen SS uniforms and headgear.

> Trivia: The SS colors were black and white, the same as worn by the Teutonic Knights.

SS-123
L = 127mm / 5"

SS-123 SS

Mocha spoon.   Obverse carries a very bold SS with high
ornamentation. Reverse maker marked RM, 800, crossed
hammers of Gebruder Petersfeldt of Berlin, founded 1848..

The Algemeine-SS or General-SS was order formed by
Hitler in March 1923 as the Strosstrupp Adolf Hitler (Shock
Troops Adolf Hitler) composed of 30 men. The NSDAP was
banned after the 9 November Putsch. Released from prison
in December 1924, in April 1925 Hitler formed a new
bodyguard called the Schutzkommando which on 9
November 1925 became the Schutzstaffel (Protective
Squad). Himmler was appointed the Reichsfuhrer-SS on 6
January 1929 and was granted, by Hitler, the status of an
independent organization under direct control of the NSDAP,
Nationalsozialistische Deutsche Arbeiterpartei, (National
Socialist German Worker's Party) in July 1934.

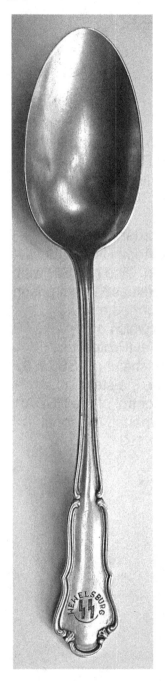

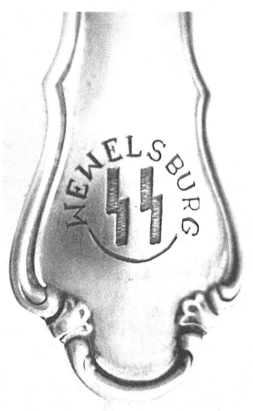

SS-124
L = 216 mm / 8 9/16"

SS-124 SS Wewelsburg,

Tablespoon. Obverse carries the SS with Wewelsburg
wrapped around the top and raised ribs, both sides,
interrupted at 1/ 3 above bottom, two lobes. Reverse carries
the maker mark of M. H. Wilkens, Bremen-Hemelingen,
founded 1810 and still active + 800 + RM.

On 27 July 1934 Himmler leased Wewelsburg castle for 100
years. The castle, one of only 3 triangular castles in the
world, was to become the ritual headquarters of the SS
Ordensburg und Reichsfuhrerschule (Cultural Relics and
Leadership School) under the command of SS General
Siegfried Taubert with a library of 12,000 volumes. SS honor
rings of deceased SS elite members were to be returned.
Himmler was to have been buried in the crypt. The spoon
has been engraved, not stamped, leading to the possibility
that this was done on site by "Niederhagen Labor Camp" ie
concentration camp detainees as the smallest KZ or
konzentracion camp collocated with the castle as a labor
source. These silver pieces were only used in the North
Tower by VIPs at this "Camelot of the SS". The castle was
the venue of various Ahnenerbe-Forschungsund
Lehrgemeinschaft - (Society for the Research and Teaching
of Ancestral Heritage) ceremonies, the body for the research
of ancestral heritage.

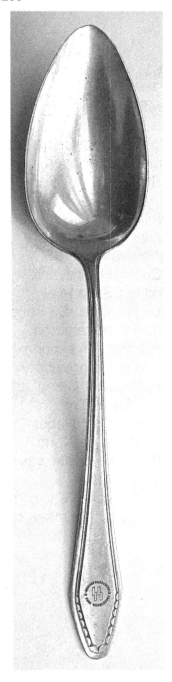

SS-125
L = 211 mm / 8 5/16"

SS-125 Wewelsburg
SS/RFS

Tablespoon. Obverse carries the SS-Reichsfuhrerschule (SS-National Leaders School at Wewelsburg emblem.. Reverse maker marked: A Centaur (an unknown maker mark) with a "20" on a square.

Himmler intended that Wewelsburg should ultimately be used as a Reichshaus der SS-Gruppenfuhrer or SS Generals' Residence, but with the outbreak of the war, it was converted into a staff college for senior SS officers and was where they would complete their education. The commandant, SS-Obergruppenfuhrer Siegfried Taubert was formerly Heydrich's chief of staff and the father-in-law of Ernst Robert Grawitz, the SS medical chief.

The Centaur is a symbol of the dark and unruly forces of nature.

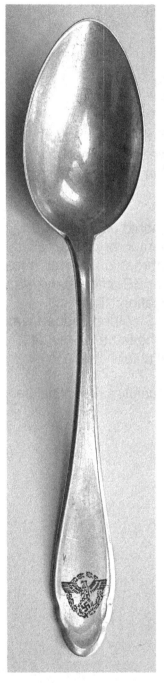

SS/P-126
L = 142 mm / 5 9/16"

283

SS/P-126 Police

Teaspoon. Obverse carries the Police eagle looking right (indicating a 'state' organization with the swastika which was added in 1933 while the reverse is maker marked: RM, '800' 'G' facing 'R'. for - Gebruder Reiner, Krumbach Bayern, founded 1914.

From Hitler's assumption of power in 1933 to 1936, his effort was to take unrestricted control of the police. In June 1936, Himmler was appointed as Chief of German Police - Chef der Deutsche Polizei. Himmler then merged the SS and the Police into a single 'State Protection Corps' or Staatsschutzkorps under Himmler as the Reichsfuhrer SS und Chef der Deutsche Polizei (RFSSuChdDP). To do this, he absorbed the police into the SS. The German Police now fell into two distinct groups: The Ordnungspolizei or Orpo, the uniformed police and the Sicherheitspolizei or Sipo, the security police. These two were folded into the RSHA - Reichssicherheitshauptamt (Reich Security Main Office) under Heydrich on 22 September 1939, just prior to the start of WWII.

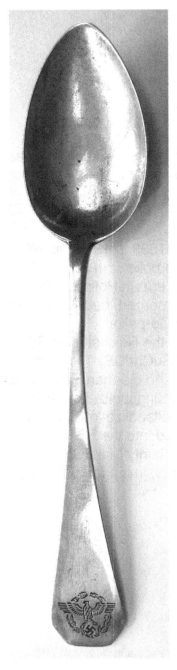

SS/P-127
L = 137 mm / 5 6/16"

SS/P-127 Police

Teaspoon. Obverse carries the police eagle looking right with swastika. Reverse carries unidentified marker mark CB, 800 RM.

The police emblem is typically a six feathered eagle. The exception was sleeve eagles which were six feathered for NCO's and enlisted men whereas the Officers and Generals sleeve eagles were 3 feathered.

OrPo Ordnungspolizei although separate from the SS their commander was Oberst-Gruppenfuhrer Kurt Daluge. They maintained a system of insignia and ranks unique to OrPo. They were the uniformed, regular police force and as a result of their green uniform, they were called the Grune Polizei (Green Police).

SiPo Sicherheitspolizei or secret police included the Gestapo (secret state police) and Kripo (criminal police) both directly under the SS.

It was Himmler's intent to wipe out the OrPo and have everyone under direct SS control.

Kasino
Polizei Praesidium
Breslau

SS/P-128
L = 214 mm / 8 7/16"

SS/P-128 Police Headquarters - Breslau
(Kasino Polizer Praesidium)

Dinner Fork. Obverse carries the police logo, the six feathered eagle looking to its left holding a mobile swastika in its talons. The left looking eagle symbolizing the Parti may be due to the items creation after being included in the SS. Reverse maker marked 'Wellner' with the elephant over 'Alpaca' followed by a 3 line impression: "Kasino' over 'Polizei Praesidium' over Breslau".

After WWI, Breslau, located on the Oder river, was in the German 'Province of Lower Selesia'. Breslau was one of the focal points for transport of victims to Auschwitz and in particular the Inspector of the Security Police and the security service's local representative of the RSHA (Reich Security Head Office) in Breslau were very active in this respect. After WWII, the Potsdam Conference assigned Breslau to Poland and it was renamed Wroclaw.

Kasino's translation is typically 'Club'.

288

POLIZEIPRÄSIDIUM
KATTOWITZ

ROSTFREI

SS/P-129
L = 202 mm / 8"

SS/P-129 Police Headquarters - Kattowitz
(PolizeiPrasidium - Kattowitz)

Tablespoon. Obverse carries 'POLIZEIPRASIDIUM over Kattowitz. Reverse marked 'Rustfrei.

Prior to W.W.I, the city of Kattowitz, being located in Prussia's upper Silesia, was German. After W.W.I, upper Silesia was granted to Poland by a League of Nations plebiscite and the cities name was changed to Katowice although the city residents had overwhelmingly voted to remain German, the rural vote carried the day for Poland. With German occupation in 1939, the city again became Kattowitz. It was during this period that the German Polizei Prasidium existed. The first Jews to be exterminated at Auschwitz (locatd in the Kattowitz district) were arrested by the Kattowitz police in September 1941. From Kattowitz, a police court-martial tribunal visited Auschwitz concentration camp every four to six weeks and passed judgement both on prisoner misconduct and hostage liquidation cases. In most cases a death sentence was pronounced. With the arrival of Red Army troops in 1945, the city reverted to Katowice.

Note: In 1953 the city was renamed Stalinogrod (Stalin's City). This was so unpopular with the residents that in 1956 it again became Katowice.

Misc: During the dismemberment of Czechoslovakia, Poland seized the area of Olsa.

LAGER
STEGSKOPF

SS/P-130
L = 210 mm / 8 4/16"

SS/P-130 LAGER STEGSKOPF
(Camp Stegskopf)

Table Fork. Obverse carries a Police logo, but here with a three feathered wing and the eagle looking to its right holding a mobile swastika in its talons. Reverse maker marked with an Wellner device composed of 'S.M.F.' in an arch over the Wellner trademark 'die' with the 4 side showing, straddled by the 'W' and 'S' for Wellner & Son over 'Alpacca' all encompassed in an oblong oval.

Stegskopf is located in the north Rheinland-Pfalz near Koblenz and was the site of both a a WWII POW camp and a training center for young German radar technicians.

The 3 feathers indicative of higher officer service?

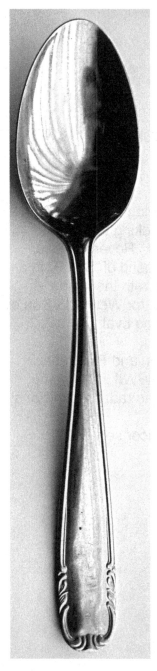

DAW
K. L. BUCHENWALD

ROSTFREI-INOX.

SS-131
L = 139 mm / 5 7/16"

SS-131   K.L.Buchenwald

Teaspoon. Obverse clear, reverse carries DAW over
K.L.BUCHENWALD, Rostfrei-Inox for Buchenwald
Concentration Camp (Konzentrationslager Buchenwald)

The KLs were founded to isolate people viewed as
"subversive dangers to the German race" and operated by
the SS, completely outside normal German law.
Buchenwald was established on Ettersberghill near Weimar,
in 1937 and eventually grew to include 140 satellite camps
or sub camps.   The main gate's wrought iron inscription
read, "Jedem das Seine" or "To Each His Own". As KL
Buchenwald was on property of the German Reich, the SS
actually purchased the camp's plants in the autumn of 1940
and founded a branch of the SS arms factory, Deutsche
Ausrustungs Werke GmbH (DAW) employing from 500 to
1,400 inmates manufacturing wood and light metal products.
The KL system was transferred to the SS Economic
Administration Main Office in March 1942 due to a decision
to engage concentration camp labor to support the war effort
oriented primarily towards the wartime requirements of the
Waffen-SS. Although not an extermination camp, the
estimated camp death rate was 18% (43,000 of the 238,380
passing through from 1937 to 1945, with an additional
13,500 sent on to extermination camps bringing the total to
24%) Prisoners were marked with triangular camp badges
of 7 colors: Red = Political, Green = Police preventive
detention, Black = Work Shy, Purple = Bible / religious, Blue
= Emigrant, Pink = Homosexual and Yellow = Race Defiler.
On 26Jan38, Himmler issued an open arrest order for all
able-bodied men "who have ascertainably refused 2 offers of
employment without justification or have begun employment
but quit it again after a brief time for no valid reason." - these
were the "Work Shy"!

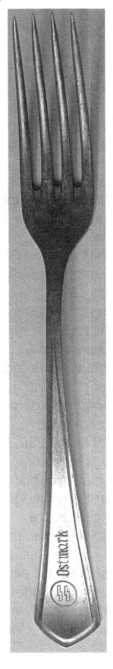

SS-132
L = 184 mm / 7 4/16"

SS-132 Totenkopfstandarte 4 Ostmark

Fork. Obverse carries "SS OSTMARK". Reverse 'Wellner' and 'Alpacca'.

The SS started staffing concentration camps in 1934. In 1936, Gruppenfuhrer Theo Eicke's Death's Head Units were combined into the SS-Totenkopfverbande. His recruiting focused on 'big sixteen year olds" directly from the Hitler Youth. Most Totenkopf (Death's Head) men were under 20, 95 percent were unmarried with few or no personal ties. They were ideally suited to Eicke's moulding to hate the prisoners. Their job being to isolate the "dangerous enemies of the state" and to "treat them rough". Any member allowing a prisoner to escape would be handed to the Gestapo. The initial SS-Totenkopfstandarte units were: #1 'Oberbayern' at Dachau, #2 'Brandenburg' at Sachesenhausen and #3 'Thuringen' at Buchenwald. After the invasion of Austria on 13 March 1938, the SS formed the fourth regiment of the Death's Head units the SS-Totenkopfstandarte 4 "Ostmark", in Linz, Austria on 1 Sept 1938. The SS-Ostmark's mission was to staff the new concentration camp at Mauthausen.

With the war, SS-Ostmark was transferred to Prague in Oct 1939 where it relieved SS-Standarte Der Führer. Then transferred to Holland June 1940 for use in the costal defense. In 1941 It was re-designated SS-Infanterie-Regiment 4 Ostmark and attached to 2. SS-Infanterie Brigade and afterward disappeared from the records on 25 Feb 1941.

SS-133
L = 140 mm / 5 1/2"

SS-133 SS Heimwehr "Danzig"

Teaspoon. Obverse carries the Danzig crest over a mobile Swastika. Reverse marked 'F.TAEGENER' RM, 800, unreadable maker mark.

SS Heimwehr "Danzig" was an SS unit established in the Free City of Danzig (today Gdańsk, Poland) before the Second World War. Originally known as Heimwehr Danzig (Danzig Home Defense), it was officially established on 20 June 1939, when the Danzig senate under Albert Forster decided to set up its own powerful, armed force. Reichsführer-SS Heinrich Himmler supported this project and sent SS Obersturmbannführer Hans Friedemann Goetze to Danzig. Goetze was the commander of the III. Sturmbann (Regiment) of the 4th SS-Totenkopfstandarte "Ostmark," established in October 1938 in Berlin-Adlersheim. On 18 August 1939, the Polish government militarily· mobilized against the German Reich. The Volksdeutsche (ethnic Germans) in Danzig "completely spontaneously" founded the 1,550-man strong Heimwehr Danzig (Danzig Militia).

On 1 September 1939, German troops attacked Poland. The SS Heimwehr Danzig fought on the German side, in the process capturing Danzig's Polish post office, an event to which Günter Grass dedicated a chapter entitled, *The Polish Post Office* in his novel *The Tin Drum*. Later, the SS-Heimwehr Danzig participated in the attack on the Danzig Westerplatte, and already was considered a part of the SS-Totenkopf Division then forming under Theodor Eicke. Later, it provided coast guard service in Danzig. On 30 September 1939, SS Heimwehr "Danzig" was dissolved, becoming a part of the 3rd SS Division Totenkopf and ceased to exist as an independent unit.

M-134

MISCELLANEOUS

M-134   HITLER Napkin Ring,
(Serviettenring)

In Hitler's State Formal (Bruckmann) pattern. The upper and lower edges have a border in a Greek Key geometric "Meander" pattern attributed to Frau Professor Gerdy Troost. Hall marked with the Reichsmark composed of a crescent moon and a crown mark indicating silver made in Germany, followed by the silver content of 925 and then a spread eagle (Maker Mark of Bruckmann of Heilbronn). This one reportedly from the Obersalzberg residence near Bertesgaden in the Alps via a 101st Airborne veteran.

'Fuhrer' Eagle and swastika with the initials AH on each side of the wreath held in the eagles talons.

Measures: 1 3/4" H X 1 5/ 8" Diameter.

NICHT
ROSTEND

M-135
L = 278 mm / 10 15/16"

M-135 Italienischer Abendessensatz
(Fuhrerbau Italian Dinner Service)

Dinner Knife. Per source, "This is a grand piece of Bruckmann table service—a dinner knife in the traditional German style with the fasces of Rome raised in high relief on the handle. RM, '800' Bruckmann eagle stamped at the top of the grip and on the blade (Nicht Rostend), "stainless." (The fasces was the emblem of authority in Fascist Italy.)

"This is a very historic piece made by the same silversmiths that made the silverware for Adolf Hitler. The purpose of this was to honor the guests among the high dignitaries who visited Germany and the NS leaders. The set of Italian service was kept in the Führerbau on the Königsplatz in Munich. This is where the most important guests to the Führer and party had their diplomatic meetings. Here is where Hitler met with Britain's Neville Chamberlain and Italy's Benito Mussolini for the famous Munich conference of September 29, 1938. This was actually a four-power conference with Edouard Daladie of France having little to say,   Many Italian dignitaries, including Count Ciano, Mussolini's son-in-law and chief of the Italian press corps and Undersecretary of State for Press and Propaganda (1934) also met there. He was also a highly placed member of the Fascist Grand Council. Many other Italian leaders of military and political fame visited the Führerbau and it was for this reason that the Italienischer Abendessensatz was created. This set of Besteck, or dinnerware, was brought out only when some of these honored guests and allies were present for dinner, and this is the one and only piece of this exceedingly rare set that we have ever seen or been able to acquire. It is much rarer by far than the Hitler silverware, again, this set was to be found in only one place and that was in Munich's Führerbau and there only."

M-136
L = 214 mm / 8 6/16"

M-136 Gastehaus Reichsparteitag

Dinner Fork. Obverse carries the logo of Nurnberg's
Gastehaus Reichsparteitag; The reverse marked
'WELLNER' 'patent, '100' in an oval and '50' in a square.

This service comes from the Gastehaus der NSDAP located
on Nurnberg's Bahnhofplatz. Hitler selected Nurnberg as
the site for the 'Party Days' because it was the "most
German of the German cities'.   The Reichspartitag (National
Party Day) started in 1925 and were held in July. The
creation of the Hitlerjugend was announced at the 2nd
Reichsparteitag on 4 July 1926. After the 1933 take over of
the German government, Reichsparteitags became the week
long Nazi Party rallies that then occurred every September
from 1933 to 1938. Each year had a theme: 1933 was
'Rally of Victory" to glorify Hitler's take over of the
Government and 1938, 'The Rally of Greater
Germany" (Annexation of Austria). The Gastehaus was for
Party and guest VIP's. This Guest House was opened in
1936 near Hitler's own Nazi Party Days hotel, the Deutscher
Hof. Both hotels were very near the central railway station.
It was a fine, very modern, air conditioned hotel with
enormous carved stone shields across the front including
one featuring an eagle clutching a swastika in its talons.
Foreign dignitaries and special guests of the Nazi Party
stayed here during Party Days. Hermann Goring was a
regular. The building remains in largely unchanged condition
today.

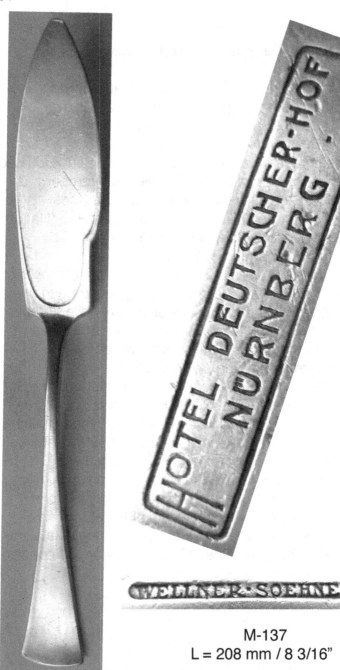

HOTEL DEUTSCHER-HOF NÜRNBERG

WELLNER-SOEHNE 60

M-137
L = 208 mm / 8 3/16"

M-137 Hotel Deutscher Hof, Nurernberg

Butter Knife. Obverse clear. Reverse machine impressed with 'Hotel Deutscher Hof Nurnberg. Maker marked Wellner Soehne 60. Typically there is one butter knife for every six place settings.

This was one of Hitler's favorites. His suite was on the 2nd floor looking on to Frauentorgraben Str. in the Altstadt close to the main railroad station. A special balcony was constructed for his use to review march buys and to be seen by the populace, primarily during the Party Days in September. Leni Riefenstahl's 'Triumph of the Will', track 2 has Hitler's arrival to the Hotel on 5 September 1934, a daytime appearance on the balcony and than after dark another appearance with a lit 'Heil Hitler' on the lower part of the balcony. After the war, his large suite was divided into 2 separate hotel rooms. The hotel was on the destruction list as it had the reputation as "Hitler's Hotel'.   It was closed in 2008 and at its demise it was listed as a 3 star hotel with 60 rooms.

Note: My wife and I visited in 2009 and it was closed for destruction whereas the Frankischer Hof hotel used by the Nazi Press Corps was remodeled into the present day Sheraton Hotel Carlton!   Interestingly, Berlin is currently reconstructing the Berliner Schloss which was demolished in 1950 by the communist government "a clearly arbitrary act: For ideological reasons." and described by H. Kissinger as, "an act of cultural retribution." How does the demolition of the Deutscher Hof differ????

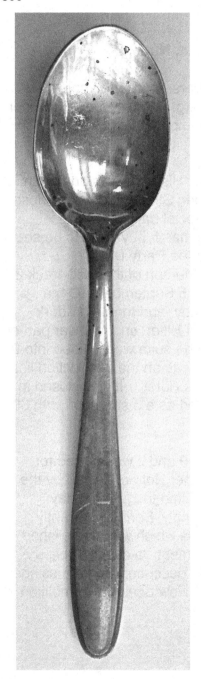

BAYER.HOF MÜNCHEN

SME 30

M-138
L = 128 mm / 5 1/16"

M-138 Bayerischer Hof Hotel, Munick

Sugar Spoon. Obverse clear. Reverse impressed with 'BAYER.HOF MUNCHEN' and maker marked with a stick figure of a man walking with a walking stick followed by BMF 30

Luxury hotels that were favored by Hitler, particularly in the earliest years, the years of struggle - Der Kampfzeit - the struggle for power - the period prior to 1933, were the Hotel Dreesen, Bad Godesberg, Hotel Kaiserhof, was Hitler's Berlin residence from 1930 to 1933. Hotel Bayerischer Hof, Munick and for Nazi Party Days, Der Deutsche Hof, Nuremberg and after the war started, the Hotel Casino, Zoppot/Sopot, N. Poland / Baltic Sea / Danzig was used as his HQ for Polish Campaign of 19-25 September 1939. After the common use of the Nazi swastika, some of the hotels saved the expense of new service utensils by such clever solutions as attaching the swastika to the underside of the tea and coffee pots.

Hitler had a weakness for fast, luxurious automobiles too. A 1925 Mercedes Benz advertisement showed Hitler about to board an enormous Benz with the headline, "Hitler leaves Landsberg Prison." In 1938, his preferred vehicle was the Mercedes 770K Pullman Convertible / Parade Car. Later he had the more enormous 6 wheeled, three axle, cross-country Mercedes G-4: The Black one was registered to the NSDAP while the Gray one license WH32288 (used for his triumphal entry into Austria via Braunau during the Anschluss on 12 March 1938, the Sudetenland October 1938 and Prague on 12 March 1939) was registered to the Liebstandarte-SS.

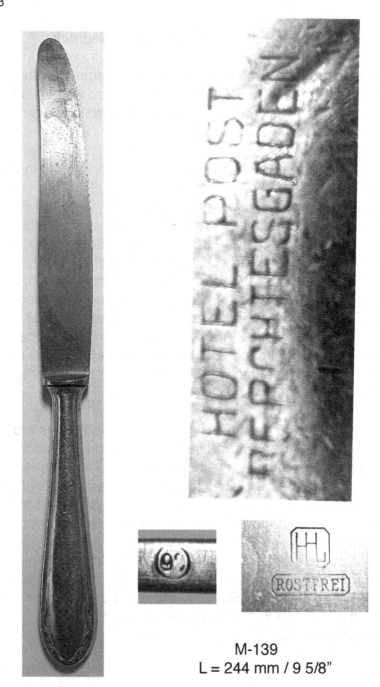

M-139
L = 244 mm / 9 5/8"

M-139   Hotel Post, Berchtesgaden

Table Knife (in poor condition). Obverse carries 'Hotel Post' over 'Bershtesgaden'. Reverse 90 HHL (Heinrich Haupt Ludenscheid Besteckfabrik)

The Post Hotel was popular with the Nazi Political, Military and Industrial hierarchy for both holidays and as a stop over during audiences with Hitler. Also a frequent stop for Eva Braun during the period that she was not allowed to stay at Haus Wachenfeld (that later became the Berghof), The Hotel Post was torn down in 2009 and will be replaced by the Hotel Edelweiss, due to open in 2010.

Berchtesgaden, located 120 kilometres (75 mi) SE of Munich and 2 Km from the Obersalzberg. had a new NS-Bahnhof which opened in 1940 with a special reception area for Hitler and his guests (now a travel agency). Obersalzberg was a mountainside retreat best known as the location of Adolf Hitler's beloved mountain residence, the Berghof and the Kehisteinhaus (Eagle's Nest - an official 50th birthday present for Hitler). Herman Goering and Martin Bormann also had residences there. Close by the Bahnfof is a tunnel were Goering tried to hide his art at the end of the war. There is a pizza shop on Schiesstattbrucke which was a Guardhouse and part of the security of the Obersalzberg.

Both Paula Hitler and Dietrich Eckart (see M-140) are buried in the Alter Friedhof (old cemetery).

The Berchtesgaden and Obersalzberg were liberated on 4 May 1945 by the U.S. 3rd Infantry Division.

Note: The 'Post' besteck of the 30's & 40's was from "HHL".
        In the 50's the service was replaced with "WMF"

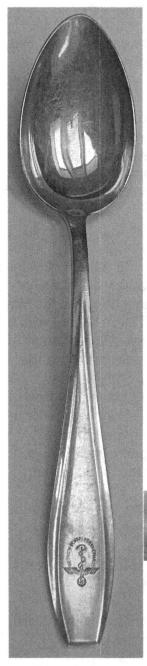

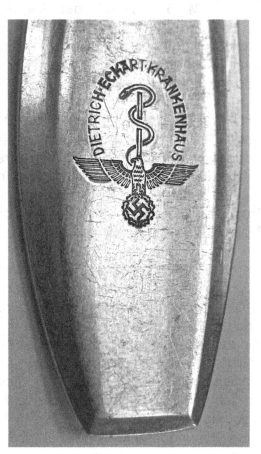

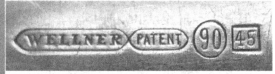

M-140
L = 213 mm / 8 6/16"

M-140 Dietrich Eckart Krankenhaus

Tablespoon. Obverse carries the logo "Dietrich Eckart Krankenhaus" which surrounds a medical staff medusa which is over an ornate eagle and swastika. The reverse: marked: "Wellner Patent 90 45".

In 1940, the Dietrich Eckart Krankenhaus (a state-of-the-art hospital) was built in Berchtesgaden on the personal order of Adolf Hitler. This is a very scarce piece of Nazi history as it is from a location named for Dietrich Eckart (B 23 Mar 1868), Hitler's mentor and the spiritual godfather of Nazism. Eckart was involved in founding the Deutsche Arbeiterpartei in 1919, later renamed the Nationalsozialistische Deutsche Arbeiterpartei (NSDAP); he was the original publisher of the NSDAP newspaper, the Völkischer Beobachter, and also wrote the lyrics of "Deutschland Erwache" (Germany Awake), which became an anthem of the Nazi party. Eckart met Adolf Hitler on 14 August 1919 and exerted considerable influence on him in the following years and is strongly believed to have established the theories and beliefs of the Nazi party. Hitler described his services to National Socialism as "inestimable" and called Eckart his "North Star". Few other people had as much influence on Hitler in his lifetime. On 9 November 1923, although seriously ill, Eckart participated in the Nazi party's failed Beer Hall Putsch; he was arrested and placed in Landsberg Prison along with Hitler and other party officials, but released shortly due to illness. He died of a heart attack in Berchtesgaden on 26 December 1923.

In addition to the hospital, Hitler dedicated the second volume of Mein Kampf to Eckart, where he praised him lavishly and also named the Waldbühne in Berlin as the "Dietrich-Eckart-Bühne" when it was opened for the 1936 Summer Olympics.

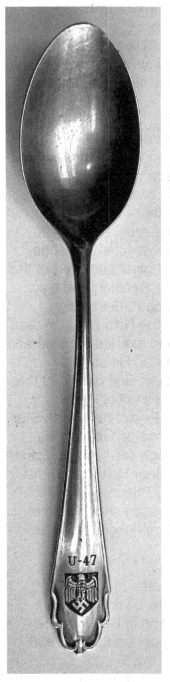

M-141
L = 160 mm / 6 5/16"

M-141 U-47

Commemorative teaspoon. Obverse carries U-47 over
Eagle looking to his right. Reverse maker marked:
Bruckmann, RM, 800 and Bruckman's eagle.

The U-47, a 753-ton type VIIB submarine was built at Kiel,
Germany and commissioned on 17 December 1938. On 13
October 1939, Cmdr. Gunther Prien, with a crew of 53, set
out in the U-47 in an attempt to attack the anchored British
fleet harbored at Scapa Flow in the Orkney Islands. In a
carefully planned operation, he made a daring penetration of
the British anchorage and sank the battleship Royal Ark on
the 14th of October 1939. Due to the poor reliability of
German torpedos, he had to fire 8 torpedoes of which only 3
functioned properly. Prien became world famous, and
resulted in his being the first Kriegsmariner awarded the
Knight's Cross of the Iron Cross by Hitler personally on 18
October 1939. Prien and the U-47 continued their success
and was the 4th highest scoring U-Boat ace credited with
sinking 195,000 tons of allied shipping. Prien was the 5th
recipient of the Oak-leaves to the Knight's Cross of the Iron
Cross on 20 Oct 1940. On 7 March 1941, while attacking a
convoy south of Iceland, the U-47 was believed to have
been sunk by the British destroyer Wolverine, killing Prien
and his crew.

Trivia: The German rank of Ka-Leut (Kapitan
Leutnant) was the rank assigned to U-Boat Captains.
The Type VII submarine was the most produced type of
war ship of all the navies in the world at 702.

314

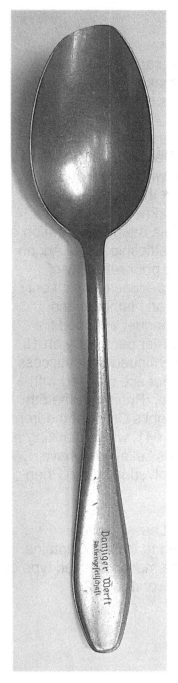

M-142
L = 210- mm / 8 1/4"

M-142 Danziger Werft

Tablespoon. Obverse marked with Danziger Werft
Aktiengesellschaft (Danzig Shipbuilding Corporation) which
was opened in 1921 and closed in 1945. The reverse is
marked 'Hansa-Rostfrei'.

At the end of WWI, this shipyard was located in the Free
State of Danzig instead of Poland due to the population
being 80 percent German and was subsequently taken over
by Germany in 1939. Located at the escape of the Vistula
River to Gdansk Gulf, the yard delivered 42 Type VII U Boats
to the Kriegsmarine between 16 December 1940 to 8
September 1943. When Danzig was taken over by the
Polish government after WWII, the shipyard became the
Gdansk Shipyard which gained international fame when
Solidarity was founded there in 1980.

Trivia: During WWII, Germany commissioned a total of
1,174 U-boats, with 702 Type VII's and suffered the
loss of 80% of their submarine crews totaling 28,751
men lost.

Rudolf Hoess, Commandant of Auschwitz wrote that
the crushed to powder remains of over 2,500,000
victims cremated at Auschwitz were dumped into the
Vistula.

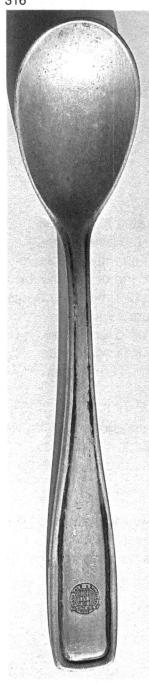

M-143
L = 139 mm / 5 7/16"

M-143 Haus der Deutschen Arbeit

Sugar spoon. This is a very rare spoon with HdD Ar.
insignia impressed on the obverse and dated 1933. On the
reverse, the Wellner name and maker mark (a die in a circle,
showing the 4 side) and "90" in a circle, "16" in a square.

Shortly after Hitler assumed power, he banned trade unions
on 2 May 1933. Per James Pool's *Hitler and His Secret
Partners*, eighty-nine union leaders were arrested and total
union assets of 184,000,000 marks were seized - enough
money to support the Nazi party for over a year. On 10 May
1933, the Deutsche Arbeitsfront (DAF) was formed by the
incorporation of all formerly free and independent trade
unions. Haus der Deutschen Arbeit may have been one of
those free and independent trade union houses that was
disbanded by the SA and "co-ordinated" by Robert Ley into
the DAF during May 1933.

A second possibility is that the HdD Ar was actually a union
hall, possibly on the national level, and not itself a union per
se as a literal translation is 'National Labor Hall'.

Note: Special group cutlery is extremely difficult to find,
especially for the smaller more exotic groups of this period.

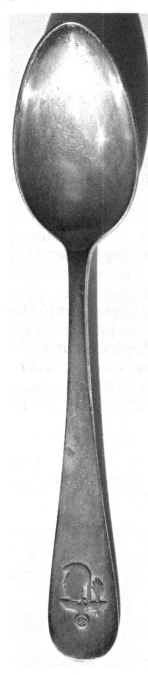

M-144
L = 110 mm / 4 5/16"

M-144   Haus der Deutschen Kunst

Mocha spoon. Obverse carries the famous 1937 "Haus der
Deutschen Kunst" logo by Richard Klein featuring a Trojan
helmet in left profile, a flaming torch and the Parteiadler. The
reverse maker marked 'B' (Bruckmann) locomotive and '90'.

The building was constructed in Munich from 1934 to 1937
following plans of Hitler's favorite architect Paul Ludwig
Troost as the Third Reich's first representational monumental
building replacing the Glaspalast, Munick's earlier art
exhibition hall which burned down in June of 1931.   Troost
died in 1934, before the laying of the foundation stone and
was declared "First master builder of the Fuhrer". The
museum, then called Haus der Deutschen Kunst ("House of
German Art"), was opened in March 1937 as a showcase for
what the Third Reich regarded as Germany's finest art and
became the venue for the greatest German art shows in
history. Hitler himself opened the "Days of German Art" 16 -
18 July 1937   The inaugural exhibition was the Große
Deutsche Kunstausstellung (Great German Art Exhibition),
which was intended as an edifying contrast to the
condemned modern art on display in the concurrent
Entartete Kunst (Degenerate Art) exhibition. In the 1937
"Official Exhibition Catalogue", P. Bruckmann ran a full page
ad with a photo of a place setting with text: "In der Gaststatte
vom HAUS DER DEUTSCHEN KUNST speist man mit
diesem BRUCKMANN-BESTECK" (In the restaurant of the
House of German Art you eat with Bruckmann cutlery)

The building survived the war as the Haus der Kunst literally
(House of Art) and is located at Prinzregentenstrasse 1 at
the southern edge of the Englischer Garten, Munich's largest
park and is included in the all day 3rd Reich Tour in Munich.

320

M-145   L = 189 mm / 7 7/16"

M-145 STAATSKASINO

Fork. Obverse carries 'STAATSKASINO' (Unknown which
Casino). Reverse marked '30' in a square and '90' in a circle
and 'Art. Krupp' the Krupp logo of a standing bear +
'BERNDORF' The short form "ART" for Arthur indicates this
fork is from before Arthur Krupp's death, as from 1938 to
1945, only 'Krupp' appeared to the left of the logo.

Note: ART KRUPP BERNDORF is the name of the
        manufacturer (Arthur Krupp AG [joint-stock company) in
        Berndorf, Austria. This firm had fabrications in Austria
        (Berndorf), Swizerland (Luzern) and Germany
        (Eßlingen).

322

M-146
L = 213 mm / 8 6/16"

M-146 Kasino Lamsdorf (Casino Lamsdorf)

Table Fork. Obverse clear. Reverse carries 'Casino' over 'Lamsdorf' with a Prussian crown between. Maker marked Berndorf Alpacca Silber II, introduced around 1880 and used fifty (!) years until 1930. Inside the diamond there are two letterings: "BMF" (with the "M" and "F" letters being fused indicating Vienna, Austria manufacture) and "ASII" (which means Alpacca Silber II, an Alpacca base covered by a double layer of silver).

The Lamsdorf 'Offizier' Casino (mess) was located at the Bahnhofs–Hotel. Casino in the military application is 'mess' or club. The forks' Prussian crown indicates it was carried over from WWI's Imperial German Army. Stalag VIII-B Lamsdorf was a notorious German Army prisoner of war camp, later renumbered Stalag-344. Located near the small town of Lamsdorf (now called Łambinowice) in Silesia. The camp initially built to house British and French prisoners in World War I. At this same location there had been a prisoner camp during the Franco-Prussian War 1870

The camp was reopened in 1939 to house Polish prisoners from the German September 1939 offensive. Later approx. 100 000 prisoners from Australia, Belgium, Great Britain, Canada, France, Greece, Italy, New Zealand, Netherlands, Poland, South Africa, Soviet Union, Yugoslavia and the United States passed through this camp. In 1941 a separate camp, Stalag VIII-F was set up close by to house Soviet prisoners. In 1943, the Lamsdorf camp was split up, and many of the prisoners (and Arbeitskommandos) were transferred to two new base camps Stalag VIII-C Sagan (modern Żagań and Stalag VIII-D Teschen (modern Český Těšín). The base camp at Lamsdorf was renumbered Stalag 344.

M-147
L = 248 mm = 9 11/16"

325

M-147 Rabbit Breeders

Dinner Knife. Obverse carries Reichsfachgruppe (Reich Specialized Group) Kaninchen Züchter's (Rabbit Breeder) logo with a raised R.D.Kl. (Reichsverband Deutscher Kleintierzuchter (Reich Association of German Small Animal Breeders). The RDKl even included bees. Reverse marked "90". Comment: The handle style is typical of Wellner and typical of Wellner, the knife does not carry a maker's mark.

In the early to mid 1930s, there were between 65 and 100 registered rabbit breeders in Germany, with their state headquarters in Berlin.

With the war, Himmler had the SS establish Angora rabbit programs at some 30 concentration camps located in Germany (with all reporting to Berlin), to produce angora wool, initially, for use for the lining of Luftwaffe flying personnel jackets, socks for U-Boat crews and when production increased, for the famous W-SS winter anoraks

SS Angora wool production: 1941 =   460Kg / 1,014#
                               1942 = 1,470kg / 3,241#
                               1943 = 2,800kg / 6,173#

This State special group silverware is extremely hard to find, especially for the smaller, more exotic groups.

Note: In many POW camps in Germany the prisoners were reduced to eating cats which were called, 'roof rabbits'

326

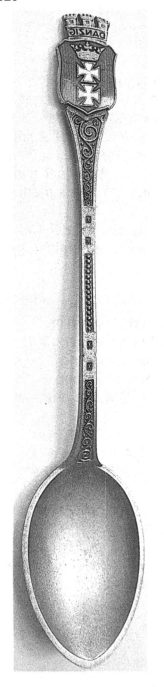

M-148
L = 117mm /
4 1/4"

M-148 Andenken (souvenir) 'DANZIG'

Small 'remembrance' spoon. Ornate obverse carries the Danzig crest with 'DANZIG' above. Reverse decorated but with no indication of material or manufacturer.

This spoon has a story! On our most recent European holiday, while visiting some old friends, my earlier book, 'Collectible Spoons of the 3rd Reich' came up. Our hostess presented this spoon to me. It had been acquired by her grandfather while he served in the Heer in Danzig as a Major in charge of a sanitaeter (medical) unit).

Major Walter Spiess was born on 3 June 1891 and spent the better part of WWII in Danzig. The spoon was brought home to Wesel Niederheim. The grand daugher, (photo left) Liebtraud Schwanke is the generous source of this spoon. Major Spiess passed away on 2 August 1971.

Note: (Major was a Staff Officer rank).

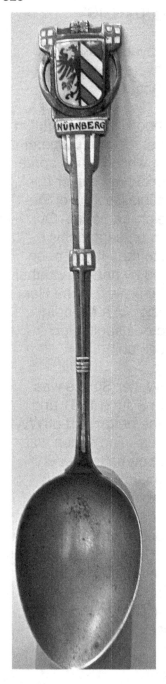

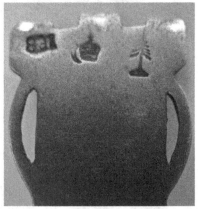

M-149 L = 120 mm / 4 3/4"

M-149 Andenken (souvenir) 'Nurnberg'

Small 'remembrance' spoon. Obverse carries the City of Nurnberg crest with 'NURNBERG' below. Reverse 800, RM, and an unidentified maker mark of a pine tree.

The collecting of souvenir spoons in Europe began about the time of the Crystal Palace Exhibition in London (1851), There developed a brisk trade in the production of souvenir spoons which travelers who visited various European cities purchased to remind them of their visit. Soon late 19th century American travelers returning from Europe brought back with them souvenir spoons from the various cities which they had visited. Two American silversmiths, both of whom had traveled extensively in Europe (M. W. Galt of Washington, DC and Seth F. Low of Salem, MA), are generally credited with being the individuals who transplanted the European "fad" (or practice) of collecting souvenir spoons to America, then these entrepreneurs proceeded to capitalize on the souvenir spoon market in the United States, see M-151.

With reference to PS-21 this spoon's Crest stripes go down to the right while the stripes on PS-21 go down to the left along with the fact that there is no city or color involved. Both M-148 and M-149 are vividly colored. This indicates to me that PS-21 is NOT an andenken as stated by only one source and that PS-21 is a Bormann item as all other sources testify.

M-150
L = 137 mm /
5 3/8"

M-150 LZ 129 Hindenburg
(Luftschiff Zeppelin #129; Registration: D-LZ 129)

Commemorative Spoon. Obverse with LZ over globe with air ship over 129. Reverse: personal engraved 'M.B.', 800 no RM. the Danish "Three Tower Mark" with year '33' (1933) and Assay Master Jens Sigsgaard 1932 - 1960.

This zeppelin, named after the late Field Marshal Paul von Hindenburg (1847–1934), President of Germany (1925–1934), was a large German commercial passenger-carrying rigid airship. The lead ship of the Hindenburg class it is the largest flying machine of any kind (803.8' long and 135.1' diameter) ever built. The airship construction started in 1931, was completed in early 1936 and flew from March 1936 until destroyed by fire 14 months later on May 6, 1937, at the end of the first North American transatlantic journey of its second season of service. The cost of a ticket between Germany and Lakehurst was US$400 (about US$5,900 in 2008 dollars The airship was operated commercially by the Deutsche Zeppelin Reederei, which was established by Hermann Göring in March, 1935 to increase Nazi influence over zeppelin operations and was jointly owned by the Luftschiffbau Zeppelin, the German Air Ministry and Deutsche Lufthansa AG, and also operated the Graf Zeppelin's last two years of commercial service to South America from 1935 to 1937. The airship's first "official" function was not to be in the commercial transatlantic passenger service for which it was designed and built, but instead as a vehicle for Nazi propaganda.

Although the passenger capacity was 72, on the last flight there were only 36 passengers with a crew of 61. Landing in Lakehurst, N.J. it was engulfed in flames, destroyed in 37 seconds with 13 passengers, 22 air crew and one ground crew perishing.

332

M-151
Teaspoon L = 136 mm / 5 3/8"
Mocha L = 108 mm / 4 1/4"

M-151 America's Swastika

The teaspoon is actually marked with 'swastika' and has arrows on the swastika's arms. The smaller, mocha spoon has a stylized (Victorian era) native American.

These 'swastika' spoons have nothing to do with Nazi Germany. For almost 1000 years the American Indians of the Southwest used the swastika as a symbol of good luck. The swastika was a respected symbol of Native America, long before it was co-opted by the Nazis. Native Americans called this symbol the whirling log or rolling log and it represented the four seasons, the four sacred mountains, and the four corners of the earth. These spoons and all of the other non-German swastika spoons were made long before Hitler adopted the swastika as the symbol of his regime. Our perception today is based upon the terrible things that were done by the NAZI's.

These spoons date to the late 19th to early 20th Century, and are remarkably well preserved, with a little tarnish and usage marks to be expected in potentially 100 year old spoons. The mania for collecting souvenir spoons in the United States began about 1890; the "souvenir spoon craze," as it was called in the newspapers at the time, lasted for nearly 30 years.

Note: The larger spoon has "Eureka Springs, Ark" engraved in the bowl. This was the final home location of Gerald K. Smith. He founded the America First Party a national socialist organization preaching nationalism and a fear of a "Jewish conspiracy."   Smith, an ordained minister, was also a prominent member of the pro Nazi organization, Silver Shirts. He also created the "Christ of the Ozarks" statue which still draws thousands to Eureka Springs.

M-152
L = 210 mm / 8 1/4"

M -152 VEB Wellner - Post Script

Soup Spoon. Reverse marked "VEB v. Wellner - 90 (in circle) - 45 (in a square).

Wellner survived the war and as a result of being located in eastern Germany, became VEB Wellner (Volkseigener Betrieb - People-owned Enterprise) or state owned workplace of the German Democratic Republic / Deutsche Demokratische Republik which existed from 1949 to 1990. Today the closed facility is: Wellner Silber GmbH at Wellner Str 61, Aue, Germany. having not survived the German reunification.

Per Wellner, the maker marks during the early VEB period used the earlier markings out of convenience. Another example of East German expediency or "why re-invent the wheel" was the continued use of the Heer's 'rain drop' pattern poncho used in 1944/45 and manufactured in the East for the 'Peoples Army' into the 50's.

The author visits the abandoned Wellner complex.

M-153
L = 128 mm / 8 3/16"

MYSTERY

M-153   Fork: GTPp

Table Fork. Obverse clear. Reverse carries a detailed eagle standing atop a wreath of oak leaves encompassing a mobile swastika and looking to his left - symbolizing the Nazi party and thus called the Parteiadler. Below is a detailed castle with an overlay of (GTPp). The maker mark is WMF (Wurttembergische Metallwarenfabrik of Geislingen, 1853 to the present), 'Patent', '90' in a square and '45' in a lozenge. An 'S' is also impressed on the throat.

Your assistance in identifying this fork's logo would be greatly appreciated!

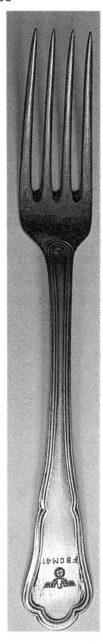

M-154
L = 208 mm / 8 3/16"

MYSTERY

M-154 Heer 'FBCM'

Table Fork. Army Mystery. Obverse carries the German
eagle looking to his right symbolizing the country / state /
military and as such was called the Reichsadler. FBCM is
the most often found maker's mark on Army cutlery and
remains a mystery as to the actual manufacturer. The
pieces can be marked on either the obverse and the reverse
with 'FBCM' and typically the year '41'.   If you can identify
the FBCM manufacturers mark, please, by all means, let me
know.

M - 155
L = 122 mm/
4 13/16"

M-155 Danish Mystery

Mocha spoon. Obverse carries a mobile swastika. Reverse an engraved letter 'J', the Danish "Three Tower Mark" with year '23' (1923), 800, no RM, and assay master mark.

This spoon raises a number of questions. The "Three Tower Mark" was instituted in 1608 as the official mark of the city of Copenhagen. In 1893 the Copenhagen Three Towers became the national mark of Denmark. The mark guarantees a silver purity of 826/1000. The number below indicates the year (four digits used until 1771, two digits after). The three towers were always marked in conjunction with the initial mark of the Assay Master (Stadsguardein). It was he who took final responsibility of guarantee. The use of both marks was discontinued by 1977. To refresh your memory, in 1884 Germany enacted a law making 800 the minimum national standard for silver. This spoon carries both 826 and 800 marks! but no RM.

The engraved letter 'J' indicates a personal spoon. In addition there is a very small Assay Master mark (at the bottom of the left top photo) of a capital 'H' with a letter 'c' between the upper H legs and the letter 'f' between the lower H legs. This is the Danish Assay Master Mark (Stadsguardein Maerker) of C. F. Heise who was assay master from 1904 to 1932.

The question: How did a 1923 spoon from Denmark get a swastika??? or more interesting - why???

Note: More Danish "Three Tower Mark" items: W-82 & M-150. They are all marked German '800' but no RM indicates these are not 'official' German silver. Germany invaded neutral Denmark at 4:15 AM on 9 April 1940. Denmark surrendered 2 hours later suffering 16 KIA.

COLLECTORS
SPECIAL NOTE AND WARNING

The SA-Standart Feldherrnhalle spoon was the only besteck
I paid for which I never received.

My method of purchase has been to identify an item of
interest offered by a known dealer (in this case, one that had
previously delivered) and to notify them of my interest and to
request a confirmation as to its price and availability. In the
interim I would research the items area of representation and
develop a one page descriptive summary as appears on the
face page. When comfortable with the item as a good
addition to my collection and when receiving the assurance
that the item was indeed available, I would notify the vender
and submit payment. This was all done for this spoon -
regrettably, I was subsequently informed some month after
payment that the spoon was not to be mine, nor indeed a
refund.

I have left the writeup opposite as the spoon is from a very
transitional time in the SA vis-a-vis the SS and as a
precautionary tale for new fellow collectors to make sure the
goods are actually in the hand of the dealer selling. ps - I'm
still awaiting restitution of my payment! Buyer beware!!!

Particularly with Florida!!!!!

OG-?? SA-Standarte Feldherrnhalle

Teaspoon, the obverse carries the SA-Feldherrnhalle (Field Marshals' Hall) emblem with the pseudo-runic SA while the reverse has the maker mark 'WMF' for Wurttembergische Metallwarenfabrik, Geislingen 1853 to the present and '90'.

The initial unit, the SA-Standarte Feldherrnhalle (a Standarte was an organization of regimental size) was formed in 1935 after the death of Ernst Röhm (Night of the Long Knives), when the SA's position as the major paramilitary formation of the NSDAP was taken over by the SS. It was made up of the most promising SA men drawn from SA units all over Germany. With headquarters in Berlin, it provided guard units for SA, State and Party Offices and as such was not a combat unit. Its units were stationed in Berlin, Krefeld, Hannover, Hattingen, Munich, Ruhr, Stettin and Stuttgart. It was one of the first units selected to enter Austria in March of 1938 during the Anschluss.

In September 1938, it was placed under the control of the Wehrmacht. In February 1939 the cadre of the unit was transferred to the Luftwaffe, forming the Luftlande-Regiment (glider infantry regiment) Feldherrnhalle, a part of the 7. Flieger-Division. The remainder of the regiment was transferred to the Heer, forming the 120. Infanterie-Regiment (mot) of the 60. Infanterie Division (mot) and 271. Infanterie-Regiment of the 93. Infanterie-Division. Thus the later Feldherrnhalle units were combat formations which drew manpower from the SA, tracing their history back to the days of the 1923 Beer Hall Putsch. As they were now in the Wehrmacht, the 'SA' was deleted from the emblem.

Material and Length Listing

PS-1 Adolf Hitler, Formal Pattern	800	146 mm
PS-2 Adolf Hitler, Curved 'AH',	800	148 mm
PS-3 Adolf Hitler, Ornamental	90	139 mm
PS-4 Adolf Hitler, Raised ribs	Alpacca	134 mm
PS-5 Eva Braun, Baroque with EB Butterfly	46?	142 mm
PS-6 Eva Braun, Parfait Spoon	90	212 mm
PS-7 Herman Goering, Coat of Arms	800	137 mm
PS-8 Goring Ribbed	800	213 mm
PS-9 Herman Goering, Reichsmarshall	800	145 mm
PS-10 Heinrich Himmler, Train Pattern	90	141 mm
PS-11 Heinrich Himmler, Script Monogram	18	138 mm
PS-12 Albert Speer, Intertwined Block AS	60	140 mm
PS-13 Helmut Weidling,	90	143 mm
PS-14 Bernard Rust,	90	210 mm

PS-15 Bernard Rust, Deutsche-Hochschule, DH	90	109 mm
PS-16 Dr. Robert Ley, Deutsche Arbeitsfront, DAF	90	216 mm
PS-17 Ernst Kaltenbrunner, Ornamental EK (Ice Tea)	100	224 mm
PS-18 Fritz Sauckel, Thuringian Eagle	90	213 mm
PS-19 Hans Frank, Governor General of Poland	90	217 mm
PS-20 Bishop Ludwig Mueller	800	217 mm
PS-21 Martin Bormann	Al	112 mm
PS-22 Joachim von Ribbentrop	925	208 mm
PS-23 Rudolf Hess	800	112 mm
PS-24 Reinhard Heydrich	100	144 mm
OG-25 NSDAP-Fraktur	800	133 mm
OG-26 NSDAP, High Leader	800	141 mm
OG-27 NSDAP / SA Early Version	Al	211 mm
OG-28 NSDAP/SA fork, very early	90	210 mm
OG-29 SA Sturmabteilung	800	145 mm
OG-30 SA Sturmabteilung	800	143 mm

OG-31 RJV / German Youth	800	135 mm
OG-32 HJ Hitler-Jugend	800	132 mm
OG-33 HJ (HitlerYouth)	800	148 mm
OG-34 HJ - RFS Leadership School	90	213 mm
OG-35 HJ - Sportschule Braunau	90	212 mm
OG-36 DAF / SdA	RF	210 mm
OG-37 DAF / SdA I. G. Farben	RF	210 mm
OG-38 DAF / SdA Bra AG	RF	210 mm
OG-39 DAF 1941	800	129 mm
OG-40 DAF Set of 7	90	NA
OG-41 Dh - alternate?	40	207 mm
OG-42 DLV German Aviation League	RF	183 mm
OG-43 DR-Deutsche Reichsbahn	800	140 mm
OG-44 DR / AH 205	800	210 mm
OG-45 DR / AH 205 detail	800	140 mm
OG-46 DR / 213	800	122 mm
OG-47 DR / Goering 243	90	216 mm
OG-48 DRK / Deutsche Rotes Kreuz	800	136 mm

OG-49 NSDStB / Student Federation	800	149 mm
OG-50 NSDStB / Student Federation	800	142 mm
OG-51 NSKK / Motor Korps - fork	90	178 mm
OG-52 NSKOV / Veterans Support	800	217 mm
OG-53 NSKOV, Basic	800	139 mm
OG-54 NSV / NS People's Welfare	800	144 mm
OG-55 RAD / Labor Service 1936	RF	217 mm
OG-56 RAD / Mess Hall Fork, 1941	RF	215 mm
OG-57 RAD Ornate	800	139 mm
OG-58 RAD Knife H.M.Z. 37	90	236 mm
OG-59 RK - New Reich Chancellery	800	210 mm
OG-60 RKB / Colonial League	800	138 mm
OG-61 RLB, Air Raid Protection	800	142 mm
OG-62 RMJ, Ministry of Justice	90	238 mm
OG-63 RNS / Food Estate	800	147 mm
W-64 Army Eagle facing right over 1942	RF	141 mm
W-65 Army Officer's Field Service	RF	NA
W-66 Army Field Service, Spork	RF	NA

W-67 Army Field Service 1943	RF	NA
W-68 Army Mess, W.S.M.42.	AL	212 mm
W-69 Army Mess, "WH"	AL	210 mm
W-70 Army Mess, 'LGK&F 39	AL	209 mm
W-71 Army Mess, B.A. F. N. 39	AL	139 mm
W-72 Army 1944Commemorative	800	142 mm
W-73 Army, JRS 41	RF	202 mm
W-74 Army H.U. - 1934 - fork	Alpacca	127 mm
W-75 Army H.U. - 1938 - knife	RF	240 mm
W-76 Army H.U. - Dug?	Pot	153 mm
W-77 Army 5./89 Marksman Award	800	213 mm
W-78 Army Fuhrer Begleit Brigade	90	138 mm
W-79 Army 1st Mountain Division	800	145 mm
W-80 Africa Corps D.AK	800	145 mm
W-81 Africa Corps D-AK, CA Krall	800	144 mm
W-82 Africa Corps, No RM	800	118 mm
W-83 Navy Mess, HHL Rustfrei	RF	212 mm
W-84 Navy Mess, Blancadur	AL	144 mm

W-85 Navy Mess, No 'M', FWW 41		RF	211 mm
W-86 Kriegsmarine Presentation		800	215 mm
W-87 Air Force Mess, Droop Tail		RF	206 mm
W-88 Air Force Mess, Oxydex		RF	210 mm
W-89 Air Force Officer's Service		plate	209 mm
W-90 Air Force Officer's Service		90	207 mm
W-91 Air Force Officer's Service		800	142 mm
W-92 Air Force Officer's Service		800	174 mm
W-93 Fliegerhorst (airfield) Julich		10	152 mm
W-94 Fliegerhorst (airfield) Staaken		90	147 mm
SS-95 SS Neusilber		NS	211 mm
SS-96 Allgemeine-SS, F.S.	Cromagan		202 mm
SS-97 Allgemeine-SS 28		800	145 mm
SS-98 Waffen-SS, DJC		800	208 mm
SS-99 Waffen SS, Alpacca		Alpacca	149 mm
SS-100 1st SS Div. LSSAH, VSF		90	208 mm
SS-101 LSSAH, Becker		90	144 mm
SS-102 LSSAH, "1941", WMF		800	138 mm

SS-103 LSSAH, LW	800	136 mm
SS-104 LSSAH, K & B	800	133 mm
SS-105 2nd SS-Pz Div, "Reich" "XX"	800	140 mm
SS-106 SS-Reich, LSF	800	139 mm
SS-107 SS-Reich, (Lightening)	Alpacca	146 mm
SS-108 SS-Reich, Textured SS	RF	138 mm
SS-109 SS-Reich, Austria - fork	RF	203 mm
SS-110 3rd SS-Div "Totenkopf"	800	141 mm
SS-111 4th SS Div "Polizei"	800	141 mm
SS-112 5th SS Div "Wiking"	RF	215 mm
SS-113 9th SS Div "Hohenstaufen"	800	133 mm
SS-114 10th SS Div "Frundsberg"	800	138 mm
SS-115 11th SS Div "Nordland"	800	145 mm
SS-116 12th SS Div "Hitlerjugend"	800	133 mm
SS-117 13th SS Regt Grp "Handshar"	800	125 mm
SS-118 15th Gren Div's 34th Reg	90	204 mm
SS-119 37th SS Cav. Div "Lutzow"	800	142 mm
SS-120 39th SS Div "Nibellungen"	800	138 mm

SS-121 SS - Raised SS	100	133 mm
SS-122 SS in a double circle	800	142 mm
SS-123 SS - Mocha Spoon	800	127 mm
SS-124 SS-Wewelsburg VIP	800	216 mm
SS-125 SS-Wewelsburg, RFS	20	211 mm
SS-126 SS/P - Police - GR	800	142 mm
SS-127 SS/P - Police - CB	800	137 mm
SS-128 SS/P - Breslau	Alpacca	213 mm
SS-129 SS/P - Kattowitz	RF	202 mm
SS-130 SS/P - Stegskopf	Alpacca	209 mm
SS-131 L. L. Buchenwald	RF	139 mm
SS-132 SS-Ostmark - fork	Alpacca	184 mm
SS-133 Helmwehr "Danzig"	800	140 mm
M-134 Adolf Hitler Napkin Ring,	925	43 mm
M-135 Fuhrerbau Italian Service	800	278 mm
M-136 Gastehaus Reichsparteitag	100	212 mm
M-137 Deutscher Hof Hotel	60	208 mm
M-138 Bayerischer Hof Hotel	30	128 mm

M-139 Hotel Post, Berchtesgaden	90	244 mm
M-140 Dietrich Eckart Krankenhaus	90	213 mm
M-141 U-47 Commemorative,	800	160 mm
M-142 Danziger Werft	RF	210 mm
M-143 Haus der Deutschen Arbeit,	90	139 mm
M-144 House of German Art, 1937	90	110 mm
M-145 Staatskasino - fork	90	188 mm
M-146 Kasino Lamsdorf	Plate	213 mm
M-147 Rabbit Breeders	90	248 mm
M-148 Danzig Andenken	?	117 mm
M-149 Nurnberg Andenken	800	120 mm
M-150 LZ 129 Hindenburg, No RM	800	137 mm
M-151 America's Swastika	925	136 mm
M-152 Wellner of East German	90	209 mm
M-153 Mystery Fork - GTPp	90	208 mm
M-154 Mystery - Army FBCM 41	RF	208 mm
M-155 Mystery - Pre 1886, No RM	800	123 mm

NA = Not Applicable

Bibliography

Angolia, John R. and Schlicht, Adolf , *Uniforms & Traditions of the German Army 1933 - 1945* , Bender Publishing, Second Printing November 1992 in 3 volumes.

Borkin, Joseph. *The Crime and Punishment of I.G.Farben*, Barnes & Noble, 1978

Buchner, Alex, *The German Infantry Handbook 1939 - 1945,* Schiffer Military History, 1991

Cameron, Norman and Stevens, R. H., translators, *Hitler's Table Talk,* Enigma Books 1988

Coates, E.J., *The U-Boat Commanders Handbook,* Thomas Publications, 1989

D'Almeida, Fabrice. *High Society in the 3rd Reich*

Davis, Brian Leigh. *Badges & Insignia of the Third Reich*, Arms and /Armour, 1992

Degrelle, Leon, *Campaign in Russia*, Institute for Historical Review, 1985

Griffith, Mark D., *"Liberated" Adolf Hitler Memorabilia,* Ulric of England, 1986

Haddock, Chase with Snyder, Charles E., *Treasure Trove, The Looting of the Third Reich.*

Hamilton, Charles, *Leader's & Personalities of the Third Reich Volume 1, 2nd Edition Bender Publishing 1996*

Hamilton, Charles, *Leader's & Personalities of the Third Reich Volume 2, First Edition* Bender Publishing 1996

Hoess, Rudolf. *Commandant of Auschwitz,* Popular Library, 1961

Jeffreys, Diarmuid. *Hell's Cartel* (I G Farben), Metropolitan Books, 2008

Johnson, Aaron L., *Hitler's Military Headquarters*, Bender Publishing, 1999

Johnson, Paul Louis, *Horses of the German Army in World War II.* Schigger Military History, 2006

Keegab, John, *Waffen SS,* Ballentine Books, 1970

Lumsden, Robin, *The Allgemeine-SS,* Osprey Publishing, 2004

Lumsden, Robin, *Himmler's Black Order 1923-45. Sutton Publishing, 1997*

McCombs, Don & Worth, Fred *World War II, 4,139 Strange and Fascinating Facts.* Wings Books, 1983

MacLean, French L. *2000 Quotes From Hitler's 1000-Year Reich,* Schiffer, 2007

Megargee, Geoffrey P. *Inside Hitler's High Command.* University Press of Kansas, 2000

Mitchel, Samuel W. *German Order of Battle* Vol.3 Stackpole Books, 2007

Piekalkiewicz, Janusz, *The German National Railway in World War II*, Schiffer Military History 2008

Pool, James *Who Financed Hitler 1919 - 1933*, Pocket Books 1997

Pool, James, *Hitler and His Secret Partners, 1933-1945. Pocket Books, 1997*

Speer, Albert. *Inside the Third Reich*, Avon Books 1970
Toland, John, *Hitler, The Pictorial Documentary of His Life,* Doubleday, 1978

von Lang, Jochen, *The Secretary* (Martin Bormann), Random House, 1979

Weitz, John, *Hitler's Diplomat* (von Ribbentrop), Ticknor & Fields, 1992

Windrow, Martin, *The Waffen-SS,* Osprey Publishing, 2004

Wistrich, Robert, *Who's Who in Nazi Germany*, Bonanza Books, 1982

Wikipedia <w> and the internet were a great help for research

Historical Addendum

Population comparison - 1939

Greater Germany	69 million
Russia	169 million
USA	131 million
UK	48 million

Military Reality

In 1933 Germany had a 100,000 man Military as prescribed by the Treaty of Versailles in 1920. The Wehrmacht was founded on 15Mar35 and the German military was expanded to 3,343,000 in 5 years under Hitler. Wehrmacht: 1Sep39 = 3,180,000, (with 2.7M Heer). Under the reintroduction of conscription in 1935, each service allotment of available recruits was: Heer 66%, Luftwaffe 25% and Kriegsmarine 9%. Actually, the Heer typically made up 75% of the Wehrmacht and within the Heer, 82% were Infantry Divisions. The Wehrmacht maxed at 9.5M (5.5M Heer) and on 9May45 still had 7.8 Million under arms with 5.3 million in the Heer).

As early as 9 November 1939, the German Army shortened their marching boots by 3 to 5 cm (1 to 2 inches) to save leather which was already in short supply. While production of the Army Officer's leather greatcoat was not prohibited until 29 February 1944.

Volkssturm's "people's army" (formed in 1944) of 6 million old men and boys armed with the true Volksgewehr / (peoples rifle)- the Italian Carcano rifle, confiscated from Italy when Italy withdrew from the war in 1943.

The War in the East

In 1941, prior to the June invasion of Russia: Germany had 3,500 tanks and German Intelligence estimated Russian tanks at 10,000.   Russia actually had 24,000.

>   Note: On 4 August 1941, Hitler commented to Colonel General Heinz Guderian regarding his estimates of Russian tank strength: "If I had known that the figures for Russian tank strength which you gave in your book were in fact the true ones, I would not - I believe - ever have started this war."

German Air Intelligence estimated Russian A/C at 10,500. Russia actually had 18,000.

German Foreign Armies East estimated Red Army at 2 Million, with war level of 4M. Actual was 4.2 Million. By invasion day, 5 Million.

In the 51st day of the invasion, Gen. Halder reported that German intelligence originally estimated Russian Forces at 200 divisions and so far had identified 360!

Germany's surprise attack on The Soviet Union started on 22 June 1941 with 3.2 Million soldiers, 2,000 aircraft, 3,350 tanks, 7,184 pieces of artillery and 750,000 horses. In 10 days they had advanced 350 miles, started the Leningrad siege on 8 Sept. 41 took Minsk in August and Kiev in Sept, reached Moscow suburbs in December. By the end of 1941, almost 1 Million Soviet jews had been murdered, all before the "Final Solution" Wannsee Conference of Jan 42.

From the invasion of Russia (Operation Barbarosa) on 22 June 41 to 8 May 45, German Losses in the East were 1,015,000 dead, 4 Million wounded and 1.3 Million missing-in-action while the Red Army suffered 14 Million casualties with over 10 Million dead. The initial casualty rate was 16 Russians for every German. In 1941, German forces took 3.5 Million Russian POW's of a ultimate total of 5 Million ,

only 1.5 Million survived the war. Over 400,000 Russian
died in the Battle for Berlin. Total estimated Russian civilian/
military killed in the East, 30 Million.

Prior to 1943, the standard German infantry division
contained some 900 assorted gasoline powered vehicles
consuming an average of 20 tons of fuel daily as well as
5,300+ horses consuming 58 tons of fodder daily.

Hitler

Versailles Treaty of 1919 - repudiated by Hitler. In 1935,
Hitler renewed conscription, founded the Luftwaffe and
started submarine production in June, 1936 renewed arms
production, and remilitarized the Rhineland (Mar) , annexed
Austria Mar 1938, annexed Sudetenland 30 Sep 38,
Annexed Czechoslovakia 15 Mar 39 and finally declared war
on Poland 1 Sep 39.

In Sept 1938, as a result of the "Munich Agreement" between
Britain, France and Germany, the North Eastern
Czechoslovakian Sudetenland was ceded to Germany,
allegedly as Hitler's last territorial claim in Europe. The
Sudetenland contained all the border fortifications
established to protect Czechoslovakia from a German
invasion. Thus Hitler had completely disarmed the Czech's
without firing a shot. On 14 March 1939 the German army
simply marched into what remained of Czechoslovakia,
unopposed and established the German Protectorate of
Bohemia & Moravia and the independent state of Slovakia
which in reality was just a puppet state of the Germans.

Per Hitler: "All administration of justice is a political activity.
Time honored commentaries have become wastepaper, the
']creative personality' of the National Socialist judge was
liberated from the mortmain of the past. The whole body of

previous interpretations of the statutes laboriously built up by German Jurists, no longer constituted precedents of value."

NAZI music: Hitler was equated to Wagner's hero Siegfried. Franz Liszt's 'Les Preludes' was always used to accompany film footage of dive bombers and also was the signature theme for the 'Sondermeldung' or "special announcements" that periodically interrupted normal radio programming to announce victories. In 1940-42, "We're Marching Against England" was the big hit. In 1944 "Dancing Together Into Heaven" was banned due to the success of allied bombing. Mozart's 'Requiem' banned as too depressing. "Fidelio' and 'William Tell' banned due to their themes of liberty triumphing over tyranny. Per Albert Speer's book 'Inside the Third Reich', he quotes Hitler, " You'll hear that (Liszt's Les Preludes) often in the near future, because it is going to be our victory fanfare for the Russian Campaign". "For each of the previous campaigns Hitler had personally chosen a musical fanfare that preceded radio announcements of striking victories."

Hitler's yacht: Built by the Blohm & Voss shipyard of Hamburg and originally launched on 15 Dec 1934 as the Versuchboot Grille (Training Boat-Cricket), in 1935 it was re-designated as the "Aviso Grille". (Dispatch or advice / intelligence boat-Cricket), and became Adolf Hitler's personal state yacht harbored at Kiel. It had an overall length of 443 feet making it the largest yacht afloat. It had three, 22.7cm cannon, 6 antiaircraft guns and 2 or 3 machine guns and a capacity of carrying 280 mines. Hitler being, "landsinning", (land-minded), and subject to seasickness, only boarded the Aviso Grille on a few occasions and shortly after the outbreak of WW2 the Aviso Grille was utilized as an auxiliary mine sweeper in the Baltic and North seas. In the autumn of 1942 the Aviso Grille was posted to Norway as a floating Staff Headquarters for the German U-boat commander stationed in Narvik. Confiscated by the British at the end of the war the Aviso Grille was eventually privately purchased and used as a cruise ship in the Mediterranean for a period of time until it was finally scrapped in the USA in 1951. As noted by Army General of Infantry Gunther Blumentritt, "Only the admirals had a happy time in this war - as Hitler knew nothing about the sea, whereas he felt he knew about land warfare."

Bandenweiler Marsch: Adolf Hitler's very own personal march played by his SS band, ONLY when Hitler was in the immediate vicinity. His 'Hail to the Chief'.

Although born a Catholic, Hitler despised religion as a crutch for the weak and believed that the idea of Christian equality protected the racially inferior of the world. (Germany was 1/ 3 Catholic and 2/ 3 rds Protestant.) Hitler privately declared that one could not be German and a Christian! Per famed psychologist Carl Jung...the decent and well-meaning German people are "intelligent enough not only to believe but to know that the God of the Germans is Wotan and not the Christian God."

Regarding the Treaty of Versailles: In 1922, Hitler said, "We do not pardon, we demand vengeance."

To manufacture the Volkswagon, Hitler had the town of Wolfsburg created. (None were ever delivered!) His nick name was Wolf, his sister was forced to change her name to "Wolf"!

Regarding his opposition: "Achievements which appear to strengthen the country do but increase their hatred. They are in permanent opposition. They are not filled with a desire to help the people, but rather by a hope which severs them from the people - the hope that the government may

361

fail in its work for the people. They are for that reason never prepared to admit the benefit resulting from any act; rather they are filled with the determination to deny on principle every success and on every success to trace the failures and the weaknesses which may possibly ensue"
AH 13 July 1934 Reichstag.

As Hitler was the Reichskanzler, actually he was Germany's 23rd Chancellor, he had a Reichskanzlei at Bischofweisen, Bavaria starting in 1937 and the Neureichskanzlei or New Chancellery in Berlin designed and built by Albert Speer in 1939 at a today's estimated cost of $ 1 billion!

As Bormann was enamored with the Obersalzberg area and to encourage Hitler's visits, he commissioned the construction of the Kehlsteinhaus (Eagle Nest) which took 13 months; its 4 mile access road cost the equivalent of $ 200 million and the 124 meter elevator, the lives of 12 construction workers. Given to Hitler for his 50th birthday.

Nazi Swastika / Flags

The Swastika is a sanskrit word meaning "well being" and is an ancient symbol used by many cultures signifying the cycle of life as well as the sun. It was also a Nordic rune and the pagan Germanic symbol for Thor, God of Adventurers. During WWI the swastika began to represent national and anti-semitic leanings in such organizations as the Thule society and other German nationalistic movements and later, assorted Freikorps groups. In the midsummer of 1920, Hitler adopted the swastika as the premier symbol of the NSDAP and in Mein Kampf, takes credit for the swastika's final presentation in red, black and white.

From Wikipedia: Nazi Flags: The Nazi party used a right-facing swastika as their symbol and the red and black colors were said to represent Blut und Boden (blood and soil). Black, white, and red were in fact the colors of the old North German Confederation flag (invented by Otto von Bismarck, based on the Prussian colors black and white). In 1871, with the foundation of the German Reich, the flag of the North German Confederation became the German Reichsflagge (Reich's flag). Black, white, and red became the colors of the nationalists through the following history (for example World War I and the Weimar Republic).

WWII Axis Powers:

Bulgaria	Croatia	Finland
Germany	Hungary	Italy
Japan	Romania	Slovakia

Ethnic Germans

Defined as considering themselves or others to be of German origin ethnically, not necessarily born or living within Germany. After WWI's dissolution of the Austrian-Hungarian Empire and the creation of Austria, the Treaty of Versailles forbid its integration into Germany. Hitler's move was to unite "all Germans". Some 6.9 million "ethnic " Germans from mostly eastern countries subsequently joined Germany's WWII effort and suffered 601,000 military deaths and 150,000 civilian deaths for a total of 751,000 or 10.8% death rate. In Aug 1941, Russian law had banished all persons of German heritage to Siberia. After WWII, some 12 million ethnic Germans were expelled by Czechoslovakia, Hungary, Rumania, Yugoslavia, Russia and Poland.

WWII European Neutrals

War is dependent on money. To quote Cicero, 106-43 B.C. "Endless money forms the sinews of war." Germany spent an estimated $ 80 billion on their military buildup between 1933 and 1939. Some 170 Infantry Divisions were created during this period. let alone an air force. Since Germany was close to bankruptcy in 1939, the money 'Gold' was taken from the defeated countries. Nazi procedure was to offer conquered countries German currency in exchange for the countries gold reserves. Belgium refused and Germany simply confiscated their gold. This helped other countries to opt for exchange. The total gold from conquered countries was in the 100's of millions if not billions of dollars in monetary gold which was converted into war material from "neutral" countries. The five European countries that remained neutral during WWII were Ireland, Portugal, Spain, Sweden and Switzerland. Their contributions to the German war effort included: Viche France (trucks), Switzerland (tools & ball bearings), Sweden (steel, iron ore & ball bearings), Rumania (oil), Spain (leather goods), Portugal (tungsten)), Turkey (chromium, being essentially the sole supplier to NAZI Germany of this key industrial metal and tobacco. By 1943, Germany had only 6 months supply of chromium). Without supplies from "neutrals", Germany could not have waged war beyond 1943! In addition, German coal paid for the problem free movement of German military equipment from Germany to Italy via the Swiss road and rail system. In 1942, Himmler stated, "The Swedes are parasites who have reaped the profits from two wars."

Nuremberg / Nurnberg War Crimes Trials

On 1 October 1946, death sentences were passed down at the Nuremberg trials for twelve of the 24 Nazi leaders tried. Goring had committed suicide on the 15th and Martin

Bormann was in absentia. The remaining 10 were executed on 16 October 1946 in the following order: 1. Joachim von Ribbentrop, Nazi Minister of Foreign Affairs 1938-1945, 2. Field Marshal Wilhelm Keitel, Head of OKW 1938-1945, 3. Ernst Kaltenbrunner, Highest surviving SS leader of RSHA 1943-1945 Central Nazi Intelligence Organ, 4. Alfred Rosenberg, Minister of Eastern Occupied Territories, 5. Hans Frank, Reich Law Leader 1935-1945 and Governor General of Poland 1939-1945, 6. Wilhelm Frick, Minister of Interior 1933-1943 and Reich Protector of Bohemia-Moravia 1943-1945, 7. Julius Streicher, Gauleiter of Franconia 1922-1945 and publisher of "Der Sturmer", 8. Fritz Sauckel, Gauleiter of Thuringia 1927-1945 and Plenipotentiary of the Nazi slave labor program 1942-1945. 9. Colonel-General Alfred Jodl, 10, Arthur Seyss-Inquart, Reich Commissioner of the Occupied Netherlands 1940-1945

Trivia: Field Marshall Keitel was the first professional soldier to be executed under the "new concept" of International law where by soldiers could no longer claim exemption due to "dutifully carrying out superior's orders".

IQ's of the tried were measured during the period of internment at Nuremberg prison.

- -

As an aside, my wife and I visit Germany every Spring, during white asparagus time. Having visited any number of antique shops in Germany, I can truthfully say that is no shortage of 3rd Reich period silverware and at very reasonable prices. To set up a small engraving operation to turn out 3rd Reich logo'd silverware would be a piece of cake except that the German authorities are quite against it. Unfortunately the same can not be said for Austria.

Comment on Hitler's Formal Service

Sets of Hitler's "formal" tableware were distributed to 6 locations. Each locations set size was believed to serve a maximum of 20 to 25 people. The cutlery (besteck) flatware pieces known to me manufactured by Bruckmann include:

Dinner spoon,	Dinner fork	Dinner knife
Luncheon spoon,	Luncheon fork	Luncheon knife
Demitasse spoon	Demitasse fork	Demitasse knife
Ice cream spoon	Desert fork	Fruit knife
Ice tea spoon	Fish fork	Fish knife
Lemon press	Oyster fork,	Napkin ring

Complimented by serving items such as: asparagus server, aspic server, pie server, sauce ladle, salad serving fork and spoon, gravy ladle, meat fork, serving spoon. pickle fork, butter knife, salt & pepper shakers etc. In addition from Wellner came serving vessels, coffee pots, tea pots, sugar bowls, creamers, casserole dish, roaster dish, gravy boat, bread plate, serving tray, warming plate, coasters, various sized serving trays. As an example, the 20 to 25 place settings at each location would typically have 6 serving vessels for such things as vegetables, mashed potatoes, stew etc. or the "Eintopf" or one-serving, compulsory meal served during the war years and therefore would need 6 serving spoons at each location for a total of 36 pieces which incidentally, were 10 inches long with a 2 inch wide bowl.

The mathematics are interesting! Bruckmann gifted 3,000 pieces of the formal ware to Hitler on his 50th birthday, 20 April 1939. Assuming each of the six locations received approximately 500 items and if a place setting could require a minimum of 18 different table items, as identified above, and with 25 place settings at each of the 6 locations equals 150 settings times 18 cutlery items equals 2,700 pieces of cutlery and 300 other items. Any additional cutlery items would add 150 to the cutlery total while reducing the servings total accordingly. This also suggests that Hitler's use of his formal tableware was limited to relatively small, intimate groups and that the meals were 'family style'. My own observation is that from anecdotal comments and common sense, between lost, damaged and as Hitler's private silver ware was in high demand as souvenirs during his life, attrition must have led to orders for replacements which indicates that the 3,000 quantity was the base number for this service.

Circle / Square marking mystery solved,

My wife and I visited the Wellner factory in Aue, Germany during the Spring of 2008. Unfortunately, we made the trip on a Sunday. Actually the day was of little consequence as the factory complex has been closed and abandoned. I have been in contact with a Wellner employee and was as mystified as I was by the square markings Wellner used. Inquiries to Aue drew helpful responses from not only the mayor but also the City museum. On our second visit to Aue in 2009, the museum director ventured that the 2 digits in a square were "style" indicators. Subsequently in discussions with an WMF employee, the same results. Therefore, I am somewhat certain that the Wellner and WMF extra numbers in the square do indicate the "style" of the tableware So the key is: The number inclosed by a circle indicates the amount of silver plate while the number inclosed in a square is the style number. Incidentally, WMF now produces silver plated tableware in 90, 100 and 150 silver weight and sterling at . 925.

Some things that are to interesting to leave out

Army:Regulation H.Dv.300/1, Truppenfuhrung (Troop
Command), a pocket sized, (4 1/4" X 6") gray
paperbound booklet of 319 pages affectionately
called Tante Frieda / "Aunt Frieda", from its abbreviated
title T.F.) postulated the basic principles of march,
attack, pursuit, defense and other military operations
for German commanders. The 1936, Berlin edition was
in Fraktur typeface!, see OG-24.

Tanks: Total German Production: I's = 1,500, II's = 2,000,
III's 5,644 (with 5,000 destroyed), IV's = 7350 (main
battle tank), V's = 6,000 and VI's = 487 for a total of
22,981!

Tanks in service on 1 September 1939: I's = 1,445, II's
= 1,226, I Command Tanks = 215, III's = 98 and IV's =
211. Of the 3,195 tanks, 1,251 were outside the
armored divisions. During September 1939 only 57
tanks were produced and only 45 IV's were produced in
all of 1939.

The Tiger I's fuel capacity was 534 liters (141 gals)
which was estimated to take it 100 Km (62 miles) on
road travel at 20 Km per hour and 50 Km (31 miles)
cross country.

The PzKw VI, the Tiger II King Tiger / Konigstiger:
Reportedly, 487 were produced. Used by the Schwere
Panzer Abteiling of the Wehrmacht and the Waffen-SS
on the Russian Front, Normandy, Holland Ardennes
and the Battle of the Bulge. Powered by a 12 cylinder
Maybach diesel, producing 700 hp, it ate 2 gallons of
fuel per mile. The Henshel turret stored 86 rounds for
the 88 mm main gun. With its massive 180 mm (7

inches) of frontal armor, the Tiger was virtually impervious to any allied fire. According to historical accounts, the front armor on the Tiger II was never breached in battle.

The 1942 Panzer Division was composed of four battalions each with 80 tanks. By mid-1943 the tank quantity was reduced to two battalions each with 50 tanks and a third battalion of tank destroyers.

At the Battle of Kursk (5-22 July 1943) the German's 700,000 men with 2,700 tanks fought the 1,000,000 Russians with 3,600 tanks. In the following 50 days, Germany lost 500,000 men and 7 panzer division (1,500 tanks)

Note: The US produced some 49,000 M4 Sherman tanks, initially with 2" of front armor and a 75 mm gun. The M4's gun could penetrate 2" of armor while German tanks could penetrate 4" to 6" of armor. The M4 was nicknamed 'Ronson' as it 'lights first time, every time" due to its gasoline fuel used by its aircraft engine. Russia produced 53,000 T-34 tanks with a 1944 run rate of 2,000 a month.

Halftracks   (Spahpanzerwagon): a 7 ton vehicle able to run at 31 MPH, carried heavy machine guns and powered by a 6 cylinder Maybach engine. Some 14,000 were built

Krauss-Maffei Sd Kfz0; 11.5 ton prime mover with a 6 cylinder Maybach HL 62TUK, water cooled engine with 140 hp moving this 22 1/2' long behemoth at 50 km/h (31 mph). 12,000+ built. Associated with the towed 88 mm FLAK gun (Flug Aberhr Kanone)

Third Reich Special Days:

1 January	Day of National Awakening
20 April	Hitler's Birthday
1 May	National Holiday of the German People
9 Nov	Day of the Fallen of the Movement

The "Blood Flag" (Blutfahne) was shown three times a year: Party Anniversary, Annual Party Rally and the 9 November 1923 Commemorative march.

Submachine Guns:

Pistol caliber submachine guns reached their zenith during WWII. The Soviet PPSh41 (PE-PE-SHA) was the dominant submachine gun with 5.5 million manufactured, the British produced 4 million Stens, the US made 1.4 million Thompson's and Germany produced 910,000 MP-40's. Within a few years, they were little more than a footnote in the arena of military small arms, having been replaced completely in concept by the intermediate size cartridge assault rifle (Sturmgewehr) introduced by Germany in the late years of the war.

Cigarets: Although they were forbidden in the Luftwaffe and Allgemeine-SS, the US military sent as many as 425 million cigarets overseas monthly. Every U.S. paratrooper carried 2 cartons of cigarets when they dropped into France on invasion day.

German Army (Heer) clothing seasons: The Winter season was from 15 September to 15 April.

Germany had 3 million deaths up till the last 9 months of the war, then 5 million more in the last 9 months for a total of 8 million.

The last Act: Did Hitler & Eva along with Goebbels &
Magda end their lives in the Tristan and Isolde search for the
realm of oneness, truth and reality, only to be achieved fully
upon the simultaneous deaths of the lovers, did they call
upon Death to make them one for ever?
Or
Did Hitler deliberately chose 30 April 1945 according to J.H.
Brennam's observation that "The Dark Initiate had remained
true to his black creed to the very last, had arranged his
affairs so that even his suicide should be a sacrificial tribute
to the Powers of Darkness. April 30 is the ancient Feast of
Beltane, the day which blends into Walpurgis Night, It is
perhaps the most important date in the whole calendar of
Satanism."

In Appreciation

As an accumulator as opposed to a collector, I am
completely reliant on my sources as to the authenticity of the
items purchased. As my primary sources, I thank the
following people and organizations for their patience,
sharing their expertise and delivering excellent besteck.

Baccardi, Ont, Canada
Brock's Inc., Decatur, Georgia
Collector's Guild Inc., Fredericton NB, Canada
Eberhardt, Matt, Nazareth, PA
Germania Int'l., Lakemont, GA
German War Booty, White Plains, NY
House of History, Seevetal, Germany
Patton, Terry, Acworth, GA
Snyder, Charles E.Jr., Bowie, MD

Thames Army Surplus, Groton, Conn
Third Reich CA, Sidney, BC Canada
Third Reich Depot, Conifer, CO
USMBOOKS, Rapid City, SD
Witte, David, Little Rock, AR
WW2GermanMilitaria, Burnaby B. C. Canada

For help on Mystery Maker's Marks:
>   Paul Raackow of Besteckliste, Berlin, Germany
>   for his kind assistance with the identification of
>   several mystery Makers Marks.

Special Note

The German War Graves commission founded in 1919
maintains some 800 graveyards in 43 countries for 1.9
million German military 'victims of war'. Some 1.5 million
WWII German military dead have not been 'clarified'.
Search is now focused in the EAST for the 250,000 German
MIA's in the Stalingrad area as well as those in the areas of
Kursk, Smolensk, the Ukraine, Poland, Estonia-Latvia-
Lithuania, the Slovakian Republic etc.

>   Donations are not US tax deductible but can be sent
>   to:
>>   Volksbund Deutsche
>>   Kriegsgraberfursorge e.V.
>>   Bundesgeschaftsstelle
>>   Werner-Hilpert-Str.2
>>   34112 Kassel
>>   Deutschland

This organization publishes illustrated brochures locating all
German military cemeteries and assists in the specific
location of the fallen for family members. The edition
covering Germany is some 100 pages. A second edition
covers France, Belgium, Luxembourg and the Netherlands.
The cemeteries are located on detailed maps with specific
directions, comments and number buried by WWI or WWII.
Due to funding constraints, all documentation is in German
only.

Final Comments

Recently I saw a Helmuth Weidling personal pattern knife handle with the maker marked 'AWS WELLNER' and the blade marked 'Henckels Zwillingwerke Solingen'. Obviously, Henckel sold knife blades to other besteck manufacturers for assembly into other manufacturers handles.

Reference Air Base Starken and Fritz Lang's 1927 film Metropolis in which the ending message of the film is "the mediator between the head and the hand must be the heart". The film addresses the conflict between management and labor that can only be resolved by a mediator with a heart. Then reference PS-16, Dr. Ley - who under Hitler's direction, eliminated the unions and placed all employers and employees into the DAF achieved Hitler's vision of "all who create with head and hand" to be in a single organization. This goes a long way to explain why Hitler (the mediator with a heart?) thought Metropolis was the greatest film produced during his life time.

Your Comment??

If you have any corrections, additions or comments, please send to my publisher for forward to me:

Trafford Publications
9045 North River Road
Suite 400
Indianapolis, Indiana 46240

Please pass to: James A. Yannes
Ref: A Guide to 3rd Reich Cutlery
Project # 191263

FINI

First of all, thanks for buying this book and especially for actually getting to the end.

As you may know, this is my 4th and my last book. The others were:

Astonishing Investment Facts and Wisdom

Astonishing Conservative Thoughts, Facts and Humor

Collectible Spoons of the 3rd Reich

And it is time to thank my beloved wife Gerda for her tireless assistance with this book and her saintly patience with the others.

Special Note: Collectible Spoons of the 3rd Reich finished in 3rd place in London's Bookseller Magazine's 2009 contest for that years most unique book title. This news was carried world-wide from the NY Times to Reuters Africa, even the Reader's Digest.

NOTES